Fodor's p

CW00351753

cape town

first edition

Excerpted from *Fodor's Southern Africa*

fodor's travel publications
new york • toronto • london • sydney • auckland

www.fodors.com

contents

maps

on the road with fodor's

THE MORE YOU KNOW BEFORE YOU GO, the better your trip will be. Cape Town's most fascinating small museum or its most innovative fish house could be just around the corner from your hotel, but if you don't know it's there, it might as well be across the globe. That's where this guidebook and our Web site, Fodors.com, come in. Our editors work hard to give you useful, on-target information. Their efforts begin with finding the best contributors—people with good judgment and broad travel experience—the people you'd poll for tips yourself if you knew them.

Myrna Robins, who writes for various newspapers and magazines, is one of South Africa's most popular food writers. Author of several cookbooks, including *Cape Flavour—A Guide to Historic Restaurants of the Cape*, she divides her time between the Atlantic seaboard suburb of Blouberg and the exquisite hamlet of McGregor in the Riviersonderend mountains.

Jennifer Stern is the content manager of the official South African Tourism Web site, www.southafrica.net, and the author of *Southern Africa on a Budget* and *Guide to Adventure Travel in Southern Africa*. In the line of duty, she has braved strange wayside pubs, dived pristine reefs, paddled beautiful rivers, walked with wildlife, and ridden mountain bikes, horses, camels and elephants all over the wilder parts of the subcontinent.

Don't Forget to Write

Keeping a travel guide fresh and up-to-date is a big job. So we love your feedback—positive and negative—and follow up on all suggestions. Contact the Pocket Cape Town editor at editors@fodors.com or c/o Fodor's, 280 Park Avenue, New York, New York 10017. And have a wonderful trip!

Karen Cure

Karen Cure
Editorial Director

Garies

R357

R27

Loeriesfontein

Klein-Doring

Hantam

Williston

N7

Sout

Nieuwoudtville

HANTAMSBERG

R63

Riet

R27

Vredendal

Vanrhynsdorp

Calvinia

R355

Fish

Strandfontein

R364

Doringbaai

Lambert's Bay

R364

Clanwilliam

Tankwa-Karoo
National Park

R354

Elands Bay

CEDARBERG

N7

Doring

Sutherland

St. Helena
Bay

R366

R27

Citrusdal

R356

Stompneusbaai

Veldrif

R399

Paternoster

Vredenburg

Piketberg

R303

Saldanha

Langebaan

R45

R311

R44

Tulbagh

Laingsburg

West Coast
National Park

R27

R307

Ceres

N1

Touws River

Darling

Malmesbury

Mamre

Wellington

Worcester

Montagu

Melkbosstrand

Paarl

N1

R43

R60

Robertson

Barrydale

Milnerton

Durbanville

Franschhoek

Genadendal

Swellendam

Cape Town

Bellville

Stellenbosch

Greyton

R319

Bredie

Muizenberg

Somerset
West

Caledon

N2

Malgas

False
Bay

R310

OVERBERG

R317

Simon's Town

R44

Hermanus

Bredasdorp

De Hoop
Nature
Reserve

Cape of
Good Hope

Stanford

Elim

Gordon's Bay

Waenhuiskrans

Kleinmond

Gansbaai

Struisbaai

N

Cape
Agulhas

L'Agulhas

ATLANTIC

OCEAN

0   60 miles

0   60 km

cape town

Victoria Basin

WATERFRONT
Penny — Clocktower
Ferry — Museum
Victoria & Alfred
Waterfront Info Centre
Alfred
Basin
West Quay
Two Oceans Aquarium
S. A. Maritime
Museum

FORESHORE

TO SEA
← POINT

M61 Main

Somerset
Prestwich
Chiappini

Waterkant
Riebeek
Waterkant

Strand
Castle St.
Hout

Longmarket
Chiappini
Rose
Church

SCHOTSCHE
KLOOF
Dorp
Upper Leeuwen
Upper Bloem

▲
Signal Hill

Pentz
Military
Lion
Bryant
Bree

Table
Mountain

Park

Victoria Basin
South Arm
South Arm
Dock

Duncan
Dock

Duncan

Coen Steytler

CENTRAL

Long St.
Loop

Burg St.
Longmarket
Dorp

Long St.
Loop
Kloof
Rheed

Queen Victoria St.
Orange St.

Adderley St.

Heerengracht

D. F. Malan
Jan Smuts

Hertzog Boulevard
Civic
Center
Old Marine

Strand
General
Post Office

Darling St.   M4

Corporation
Caledon
Albertus
Barrack
Commercial
Roeland

Parliament St.
Government Ave.
St. John's
Hope
Hatfield

■ **District**
Six
Museum

Buitenkant
Canterbury
Wesley

Robben
Island

0   500 yards
0   500 meters

N1

Oswald Pirow

cape town

In This Chapter

introducing
cape town

CAPETONIANS TEND TO LOOK WITH PITY on those who don't have the
good fortune to live in their Eden. Their attitude is
understandable—Cape Town is indeed one of the world's fairest
cities. Backed by Table Mountain, the city presides over a coastline
of unsurpassed beauty: of mountains cascading into the sea,
miles of beaches, and 17th-century wineries snoozing under giant
oaks. Modern South Africa was born here, and the city is filled
with historic reminders of its three centuries as the sea link
between Europe and the East.

A stroll through the lovely city center reveals Cape Town's three
centuries as the sea link between Europe and the East. Elegant
Cape Dutch buildings with their whitewashed gables abut
imposing monuments to Britain's imperial legacy. In the Bo-
Kaap neighborhood the call to prayer echoes from minarets
while the sweet tang of Malay curry wafts through the cobbled
streets. And everywhere, whether you're eating outdoors at one
of the country's best restaurants or sipping wine atop Table
Mountain, you sense—correctly—that this is South Africa's
most urbane, civilized city.

As impressive as all this is, what you will ultimately recall about
Cape Town is the sheer grandeur of its setting—Table Mountain
rising above the city, the sweep of the bay, and mountains
cascading into the sea. You will likely spend more time
marveling at the views than anything else.

The city lies at the northern end of the Cape Peninsula, a 75-km (44-mi) tail of mountains that hangs down from the tip of Africa, ending at the Cape of Good Hope. Drive 15 minutes in any direction, and lose yourself in a stunning landscape of 18th-century Cape Dutch manors, historic wineries, and white-sand beaches backed by sheer mountains. Francis Drake wasn't exaggerating when he said this was "the fairest Cape we saw in the whole circumference of the earth," and he would have little cause to change his opinion today. You could spend a week exploring just the city and peninsula—and a lifetime discovering the nearby wonders of the Western Cape, including the Winelands, one of the great highlights of a trip to South Africa.

Capetonians know they have it good and look with condescending sympathy on those with the misfortune of living elsewhere. On weekends they hike, sail, and bike in their African Eden. At night they congregate at the city's fine restaurants, fortified with the Cape wine that plays such an integral role in the city's life. Laid-back Cape Town has none of the frenetic energy of hard-nosed Johannesburg. Maybe that's because Cape Town doesn't need to unearth its treasures—the beauty of the place is right in front of you as soon as you roll out of bed.

In this respect the city is likened to San Francisco, but Cape Town has what San Francisco can never have—history and the mountain. Table Mountain is key to Cape Town's identity. It dominates the city in a way that's difficult to comprehend until you visit. In the afternoon, when creeping fingers of clouds spill over the mountain and reach toward the city, the whole town seems to shiver and hold its breath. Depending on which side of the mountain you live, it even dictates when the sun will rise and set.

Indeed, the city owes its very existence to the mountain. The freshwater streams running off its slopes were what first prompted early explorers to anchor here. In 1652 Jan van

Riebeeck and 90 Dutch settlers established a revictualing station for ships of the Dutch East India Company (VOC) on the long voyage east. The settlement represented the first European toehold in South Africa, and Cape Town is still sometimes called the Mother City.

Those first Dutch settlers soon ventured into the interior to establish their own farms, and 140 years later the settlement supported a population of 20,000 whites as well as 25,000 slaves brought from distant lands like Java, Madagascar, and Guinea. Its position on the strategic cusp of Africa, however, meant the colony never enjoyed any real stability. The British, entangled in a global dogfight with Napoléon, occupied the Cape twice, first in 1795 and then more permanently in 1806. With them they brought additional slaves from Ceylon, India, and the Philippines. Destroyed or assimilated in this colonial expansion were the indigenous Khoikhoi (Hottentots), who once herded their cattle here and foraged along the coast.

For visitors used to hearing about South Africa's problems in black and white, Cape Town might come as a surprise—the city is black, white, and colored. Today more than 1 million coloreds—the term used to describe people of mixed race, Malay, Indian, or of Khoikhoi or slave descent—live in the city and give it a distinct spice.

Perhaps the greatest celebration of this colored culture is the annual Coon Carnival, when thousands of wild celebrants take to the streets in vibrant costumes to sing *moppies* (vaudeville-style songs), accompanied by banjos, drums, and whistles. The carnival is the most visible reminder of a way of life that saw its finest flowering in District Six, a predominantly colored but truly multiracial neighborhood on the fringes of the city center whose destruction was a tragic result of apartheid in Cape Town. District Six was a living festival of music and soul, a vibrant community bound by poverty, hope, and sheer joie de vivre. In 1966 the Nationalist government invoked the Group Areas Act,

Come Again?

Listed below are some words you should know.

BAKKIE: pickup truck

BONNET: hood (of a car)

BOOT: trunk (of a car)

BOTTLE STORE: liquor store

BRA/BRU/MY BRA: brother, term of affection or familiarity

DAGGA/ZOL: marijuana

JOL: a party or night on the town

HOWZIT?: literally, "How are you?" but used as a general greeting

IZIT?: Really?

JUST NOW: recently or any time in the near or distant future

LEKKER: nice

PAVEMENT: sidewalk

PETROL: gasoline

ROBOT: traffic light

SHAME: "How cute" or "What a pity"

SHEBEEN: township bar

SIS: gross, disgusting

SISI OR USISI: sister, term of affection or respect

SKOLLIE/SKEBENGA/TSOTSI: thug, ruffian

TAKKIE: sneaker

TOYI-TOYI: to dance in protest

VELD: open countryside

YEBO: yes or hello

rezoned District Six a whites-only area, and razed it. The scars of that event still run deep. A new museum seeks to recapture the mood of the lost community, and a move is afoot to build low-cost housing in the area, although it has been suggested that it be turned into some kind of living monument, instead.

Other legacies of apartheid fester. Each year for decades, thousands of blacks have streamed to the Cape in search of work, food, and a better life. They end up in the squatter camps of Crossroads and Khayelitsha, names that once flickered across TV screens around the globe. Many visitors never see this side of South Africa, but as you drive into town along the N2 from the airport, you can't miss the pitiful shacks built on shifting dunes as far as the eye can see—a sobering contrast to the first-world luxury of the city center. A tour of these areas offers a glimpse of the old South Africa—and the enormous challenges facing the new one.

PLEASURES AND PASTIMES

Beaches

The Cape's beaches on both the Atlantic and False Bay sides are truly legendary. They stretch endlessly, and you can walk for miles without seeing a fast-food outlet or cool-drink stand. What you're likely to see are seagulls, dolphins, penguins, and whales (in season). Forget swimming in the Atlantic—even a dip will freeze your toes. The "in" crowd flocks to Clifton, a must for sunbathers. Although Camps Bay, Llandudno, and Sandy Bay have their attractions, if it's swimming you're into, take yourself to the warmer waters of St. James, Kalk Bay, Fish Hoek, and Simonstown, all on the False Bay side. Windsurfers congregate at Blouberg, where several competitions are held. Don't miss Boulders or Seaforth for snorkeling among great rocks in secluded coves and pools.

Cricket

White South Africans are crazy about cricket—during international matches you'll often find crowds gathered in pubs around large-screen televisions. A major push is under way to introduce cricket into black communities, but it remains essentially a white sport.

Cycling

You can do a gentle cycle through the Winelands of the Cape or to the scenic Cape Point. If you're a keen cyclist, the Argus Cycle Tour, in Cape Town in March, is the biggest individually timed event in the world. It's 115 km (about 70 mi) long, and contestants number more than 30,000.

Dining

Fresh seafood is abundant in Cape Town and the surrounding areas. Varieties include plump Knysna oysters and local lobsters, known as crayfish. All of South African has a love affair with Indian cuisine, first brought here by indentured laborers in the 19th century. Samosas and curries appear on almost every menu. South Africa's own Cape Malay cuisine, most evident in the Cape, is a centuries-old blend of recipes brought by early Dutch settlers and slaves transported from the Dutch East Indies. The cuisine is characterized by mild, fruity curries and the use of aromatic spices. Essential in the ubiquitous South African barbecue, or *braai*, are *boerewors* (sausages). Also used are fish, crayfish tails, spicy *sosaties* (kebabs), *pap en sous* (cornmeal), and *potjiekos* (stew). And, of course, no braai is complete without beer.

Flora

Nowhere is this blessing of nature more evident than in the Cape, home to the smallest and richest of the world's six floral kingdoms. More than 8,500 species of plants grow in the province, of which 5,000 are endemic. Much of the Cape vegetation consists of *fynbos* (pronounced "*feign*-boss"), hardy, thin-leaved plants ideally suited to the Cape environment. Proteas, including the magnificent king protea, are examples of fynbos.

History

Wherever you are, there's history in the air. Take a cultural tour of the townships and Bo-Kaap to see communities still struggling to emerge from the yoke of apartheid. Take a tour of Robben Island, where Nelson Mandela and thousands of other political prisoners were imprisoned for so many long years. Cape Town's small, so walking tours are easy, and you can pack in a lot in just a few hours.

Markets

Cape Town has the best markets in the country—informal, creative, artistic, with a good selection of the usual tatty or really splendid African curios. The Waterfront markets are tremendous, and serious goody hunters might strike gold at the Greenpoint open-air market on a Sunday. Greenmarket Square's terrific: Look out for the special rubber-tire sandals. The Rondebosch Park Craft Market, on the first Saturday of the month, has unusual items, as does the Constantia Market, held on summer weekends. Read the papers for up-to-date listings on these and other ephemeral markets, such as the Observatory Holistic Lifestyle Fair, held on the first Sunday of the month.

Outdoor Activities

Cape Town is the adventure capital of South Africa, with great surfing, wonderful diving, world-class climbing, excellent paragliding and hang gliding, horseback riding along lonely beaches or bright green vineyards, and hectic single-track mountain biking as well as some fun and easy biking trails, sailing, kite flying, and, of course, hiking and walking along the slopes of Table Mountain or the edge of the sea. Or for something totally different, hurtle earthward in a tandem sky dive with Table Mountain as a backdrop, or fly upside down in an aerobatic plane. You'll be spoiled by all the choices.

Picnics

Cape Town is the ultimate picnic land. Pack a basket and head off to Rondevlei to bird-watch or to the top of Table Mountain to enjoy gorgeous views. Capetonians love evening beach picnics at the end of long summer days. Choose Bakoven, Clifton, or Llandudno and watch the pink sun turn crimson before it slips below the horizon.

Rugby

Although long associated with white Afrikaners, rugby became a unifying force in South Africa during the 1995 Rugby World Cup, when South Africa's Springboks beat the New Zealand All Blacks in the final, sparking a nationwide celebration among all races. The audience is still mostly white, but it is changing. The national side, too, is slowly losing its pale complexion—first with the legendary stalwart, Chester Williams, and then the brilliant and diminutive Breyton Paulse, who was shortly followed by fullback Conrad Jantjies. Rugby is taken very, very seriously in South Africa and inspires a devotion bordering on religion. In addition to a series of international matches staged each year, the rugby calendar is notable for the Currie Cup, played to decide the best provincial team in the country.

Scuba Diving

Kelp forests off Cape Town provide icy diving. There are dive shops, schools, and resorts all along the coast.

Soccer

If rugby is what gets white South African men out of bed on a weekend, soccer does the same for their black counterparts. There is an increasing overlap, but each game is still quite culture specific. And soccer is taken every bit as seriously as rugby.

Surfing

In the cult movie *Endless Summer*, globe-trotting surfers discovered the perfect wave at Cape St. Francis, near Port Elizabeth. South Africa is one of the major surfing countries in the world, with South Africans figuring prominently on the professional circuit. Durban is probably the center of wave mania, but beaches around Cape Town and up the West Coast (Elands Bay, in particular) are popular, too, although you need a good wet suit to survive the cold water.

Wine

Forgotten during the years of international sanctions, South African wines are only now getting the recognition they deserve. The quality and range of wines available are excellent. Pinotage, for one, is a uniquely South African blend of pinot noir and cinsault (or cinsaut) grapes (cinsault is known in South Africa as Hermitage). Equally appealing are the low, low prices: Expect to pay no more than $10 for a fantastic bottle of wine and $20 for a superb one. Unfortunately, wine prices are almost doubled in restaurants but are still pretty reasonable.

QUICK TOURS

TWO-DAY TOUR

On your first day take an early morning city walk to see the sights or take a half-day city tour. You will see the **COMPANY'S**

GARDENS, the **CASTLE OF GOOD HOPE, CITY HALL,** the **BO-KAAP,** and other historical highlights.

For lunch go to the **V&A WATERFRONT** and eat at one of the outside restaurants if the weather's good, inside if it's not. Visit the various waterfront attractions, including the **AQUARIUM** (a must) and the **SAS SOMERSET.** If you don't dine at the Green Dolphin and listen to terrific jazz, then move away from the waterfront and go uptown.

Perhaps have dinner in one of the city's many excellent restaurants and then go to the theater, ballet, or opera at the **ARTSCAPE THEATRE COMPLEX** or at the **BAXTER THEATRE.** For a real taste of contemporary African–New Age Cape Town fusion, go to the Drum Cafe, on Glynn Street, to watch a performance and maybe join in a drum circle.

The next morning take a **ROBBEN ISLAND** tour, which takes 3½ hours. On your return go straight to the **LOWER CABLEWAY** and ride to the summit of **TABLE MOUNTAIN.** Have lunch in the restaurant and hike one of the trails—walks can last from a few minutes to a few hours.

When you come down from the mountain, drive to **CAMPS BAY** and dine at a beach-view restaurant. Then kick off your shoes and walk on the beach. To round out the evening, you might want to take in a show at the Playhouse Theatre in Camps Bay.

FIVE-DAY TOUR
Spend the first day or two exploring Cape Town. There's a lot to see. Pop into museums and galleries, visit **BO-KAAP,** and wander around this old Cape Malay area with its cobblestone streets and quaint buildings. On the afternoon of the second day browse along the waterfront.

On the morning of Day 3 explore **ROBBEN ISLAND** and, on your return, lunch at the waterfront. In the afternoon you might visit the castle or have high tea at the **MOUNT NELSON HOTEL.** In the evening head out to the vibey suburb of Observatory for dinner, and then wander down Lower Main Road, perhaps popping in for a drink or late-night coffee at a café.

On Day 4 drive out to **CONSTANTIA WINELANDS**. Visit the estates, enjoy the countryside, do a little wine tasting, have lunch, and then in the afternoon drive over Constantia Nek to Hout Bay. Go to the harbor and take an early afternoon cruise to Seal Island. For a more adventurous activity, maybe admire the sunset from the back of a horse on Noordhoek or Hout Bay Beach or from a kayak out at sea. If the conditions are right, you could do a tandem paraglider flight off Lion's Head, landing at the popular La Med just in time for cocktails overlooking the beach. Even if you don't paraglide in here, have dinner on this side of the mountain, at Greenpoint, Sea Point, or Camps Bay.

Day Five is penguin day. You simply have to take the trek—it's a fairly long drive—and wend your way along the False Bay coast to **BOULDERS BEACH,** in Cape Peninsula National Park, where you'll find Cape penguins in profusion. This is one of the few mainland sites in the world where these comical little creatures live and breed. Then go on a little farther for a seafood lunch at Millers Point. In the afternoon grab your map and follow the road to the Cape of Good Hope, part of the national park (there's a separate admission fee), and, of course, Cape Point. You can take the steep walk to the point, or take the funicular. It looks as if this is where the Indian and Atlantic oceans meet— sometimes there is even a line of foam stretching out to sea— but of course it's not. No matter, it's a dramatic spot.

In This Chapter

Updated by Jennifer Stern

here and there

CAPE TOWN IS SURPRISINGLY SMALL. The area between Table Mountain
and Table Bay, including the city center and the nearby suburbs,
is known as the City Bowl. In the city center an orderly street grid
and the constant view of Table Mountain make it almost impossible
to get lost. Major arteries running toward the mountain from the
sea are Adderley, Loop, and Long streets; among the major cross
streets are Strand, Longmarket, and Wale, which is alternately
written as WALE ST. and WAALST on signs. The heart of the historic
city is Government Avenue, a pedestrian mall at the top of Adderley
Street. St. George's Mall, another major pedestrian thoroughfare,
runs the length of commercial Cape Town.

Few other cities in the world have grown the way Cape Town has.
Take a good look at the street names. Strand and Waterkant
(meaning "waterside") streets are now far from the sea.
However, when they were named, they were right on the beach.
An enormous program of dumping rubble into the ocean
extended the city by a good few square miles. Almost all the city
on the seaward side of Strand and Waterkant is part of the
reclaimed area of the city known as the Foreshore.

Once you leave the city center, orienting yourself can be tricky. As
you face Table Mountain from the city, the distinctive mountain
on your left is Devil's Peak; on the right are Signal Hill and Lion's
Head. Signal Hill takes its name from a gun fired there every day
at noon. If you look carefully, you will see that Signal Hill forms
the rump of a reclining lion, while the maned Lion's Head looks
south past Table Mountain (best seen from the N1 driving in to

town). On the other side of Signal Hill and Lion's Head lie the
Atlantic communities of Sea Point, Clifton, and Camps Bay.
Heading the other way, around Devil's Peak, you come to Cape
Town's exclusive southern suburbs—Rondebosch, Newlands,
Claremont, and Constantia. The happening Waterfront lies
north of the City Bowl on the other side of the horrendous
freeways that separate the docks from downtown.

The Cape Peninsula, much of which is included in the newly
proclaimed Cape Peninsula National Park (CPNP), extends 40
km (25 mi) below the city. The park comprises Table Mountain,
most of the high-lying land on the Peninsula Mountain chain that
runs down the center of the peninsula, what used to be known as
the Cape Point Nature Reserve, and Boulders Beach. The steep
mountain slopes leave little room for settlement in the narrow
shelf next to the sea. The east side of the peninsula is washed by
the waters of False Bay. Here, connected by a coastal road and
railway line, lie the suburbs of Muizenberg, St. James, Kalk Bay,
and Fish Hoek, as well as the naval base at historic Simonstown.
The western shores of the peninsula are wilder and emptier,
pounded by huge Atlantic swells. In addition to the tiny hamlets
of Scarborough, Kommetjie, Noordhoek, and Llandudno, you'll
find the fishing port of Hout Bay.

TABLE MOUNTAIN

Along with Victoria Falls on the border of Zimbabwe and Zambia,
Table Mountain is one of southern Africa's most beautiful and
impressive natural wonders. The mountain rises more than 3,500
ft above the city, its flat top visible to sailors 65 km (40 mi) out to
sea. In summer, when the southeaster blows, moist air from False
Bay funnels over the mountain, condensing in the colder, higher
air to form a tablecloth of cloud. Legend attributes this low-lying
cloud to a pipe-smoking contest between the devil and Jan van
Hunks, a pirate who settled on Devil's Peak. The devil lost, and
the cloud serves to remind him of his defeat.

The first recorded ascent of Table Mountain was made in 1503 by Portuguese admiral Antonio de Saldanha, who wanted to get a better sense of the topography of the Cape Peninsula. He couldn't have asked for a better view. In one direction you look down on today's city, cradled between Lion's Head and Devil's Peak. In another you see the crescent of sand at Camps Bay, sandwiched between the sea and the granite faces of the Twelve Apostles. Farther south the peninsula trails off toward the Cape of Good Hope, its mountains forming a ragged spine between False Bay and the empty vastness of the Atlantic. No matter where you look, you just can't get over how high you feel.

Despite being virtually surrounded by the city, Table Mountain is a remarkably unspoiled wilderness. Most of the Cape Peninsula's 2,200 species of flora are found on the mountain, and there are about as many plant species in the Cape Peninsula as there are in the whole of North America and Europe combined, including magnificent wild indigenous flowers, known as *fynbos*. The best time to see the mountain in bloom is between September and March. Long gone are the days when Cape lions, zebras, and hyenas roamed the mountain, but you can still glimpse *grysboks* (small antelopes), baboons, and rabbitlike *dassies* (rock hyraxes), who congregate in large numbers near the Upper Cable Station.

Atop the mountain, well-marked trails offering 10- to 40-minute jaunts crisscross the western Table near the Cableway. Many other trails lead to the other side of Platteklip Gorge and into the mountain's catchment area, with reservoirs, hidden streams, and more incredible views. Be aware, though, that weather on the mountain can change quickly. Even if you're making only a short visit, take a sweater. If you're planning an extended hike, carry water, plenty of warm clothing, and a mobile phone.

During the warm summer months Capetonians are fond of taking picnic baskets up the mountain. The best time to do this is after 5: some say sipping a glass of chilled Cape wine while watching the sun set from Table Mountain is one of life's great joys. You can also eat at the large self-service restaurant, whose eclectic buffet includes some South African–style food, like Malay curry, and a range of Mediterranean appetizers. The hot breakfasts are great. The smaller bistro serves cocktails, coffees, and pastries. The restaurant is open from 8:30 to 3:30 and the bistro from 10 until the last cable car. Both restaurants have a good wine list with local wines predominating. For noshers, there's a fast-food kiosk.

If you're feeling adventurous, try a rappel from the mountaintop—it's only 370 ft, but you're hanging out over 3,300 ft of air. You have only two ways of reaching the top of the mountain: walk, or take the Cableway.

Riding the Cableway

Cable cars take from three to five minutes to reach the summit. There used to be terrible congestion at the Lower Cable Station, but the building of the new **CABLEWAY**, with two large, wheelchair-friendly revolving cars that give a 180-degree view, has eased things somewhat. You can't prebook for the cable car, but the longest you'll have to wait is about an hour, and then only in peak season (December 15–January 15). Several tour operators include a trip up the mountain in their schedules. *Tafelberg Rd., tel. 021/424–8181, www.tablemountain.co.za. R85 round-trip, R45 one-way (depending on season). Dec.–May, daily 8:30 AM–9 PM; June–Aug., daily 8:30–6; Sept.–Nov., daily 8–7:30.*

The Lower Cableway lies on the slopes of Table Mountain near its western end. It's a long way from the city on foot, and you're better off traveling by car, taxi, or riki (a slow, low-tech minibus). To get there from the City Bowl, take Buitengracht Street toward the mountain. Once you cross Camp Street, Buitengracht becomes Kloof Nek Road. Follow Kloof Nek Road through the residential neighborhood of Gardens to a traffic circle; turn left on Tafelberg Road and follow signs to the Lower Cableway.

A taxi from the city center to the Lower Cableway (one-way) costs about R70–R90, and a riki costs R15–R20 per person, but they are only available during the week.

Walking Up the Mountain

More than 300 walking trails wend their way up the mountain, but the only easy route up the front section is via Platteklip Gorge. You can start at the Lower Cable Station, but remember that you need to walk about three to four km (2–2½ mi) to the left (east) before heading up. It is easier but slightly less scenic to walk along Tafelberg Road until the PLATTEKLOOF GORGE sign and then head up. Once on the right path you shouldn't get lost. There is no water in Platteklip Gorge; you must take at least 2 liters (½ gallon) of water per person. Table Mountain can be dangerous if you're not familiar with the terrain. Many paths that look like good routes off the mountain end in treacherous cliffs. Do not underestimate this mountain. It may be in the middle of a city, but it is not a genteel town park. Always take warm clothes and a mobile phone, and let someone know of your plan. The mountain is quite safe if you stick to known paths. If you are on the mountain and the weather changes dramatically (heavy rain, mist) and you can't tell where you are, just sit tight—you will be rescued as soon as the weather permits. Walking around in the mist is quite dangerous. There are several routes from Kirstenbosch National Botanic Gardens that are wonderful, easy, and scenic but that take you to a section of the mountain that is far from the front table and the cable station. If you're prepared to go the distance, you can do the very beautiful, but quite long and challenging walk from the top of the Kirstenbosch routes to the front table.

CAPE ECO TRAILS (tel. 021/785–5511, www.capetrails.com) has guided walks to the top and all over the mountain. Expect to pay R200 to R600 per person, depending on group size. A one-way cable-car ride may be included.

THE CITY CENTER

Numbers in the text correspond to numbers in the margin and on the Cape Town map.

A Good Walk

Begin your walk at **CAPE TOWN TOURISM'S INFORMATION OFFICE** ①, on the corner of Burg and Castle streets. At no time during the walk will you be more than 15 minutes from this starting point. Head down Castle and turn right onto **ADDERLEY STREET** ②, directly opposite the **GOLDEN ACRE** ③ shopping center. Turn left on Darling Street and head toward the **CASTLE OF GOOD HOPE** ④ and the **GRAND PARADE** ⑤. Just across the way is the beautiful **CITY HALL** ⑥. Retrace your steps toward Adderley Street, turning left one block before you get there onto Parliament Street to reach the austere **GROOTE KERK** ⑦. The Groote Kerk faces Church Square, now a parking lot, where churchgoers used to unharness their oxen. On the skinny traffic island in the middle of Spin Street is a concrete plaque marking the **SLAVE TREE** ⑧. A brass plaque commemorating the slave tree and a cross section of the tree itself are on display in the **SOUTH AFRICAN CULTURAL HISTORY MUSEUM** ⑨, next door on Adderley Street. Here Adderley swings to the right to become Wale Street (Waalstraat), but if you continue straight on, you'll be walking up Government Avenue, a wide and attractive squirrel-filled, tree-lined walkway that leads past many of the country's most important institutions and museums. On your right is the **SOUTH AFRICAN LIBRARY** ⑩, the oldest in the country, and **COMPANY'S GARDENS** ⑪. This is a great place to sit and watch the world go by. Continue along Government Avenue, and walk past Parliament to the **TUYNHUYS** ⑫. The **SOUTH AFRICAN NATIONAL GALLERY** ⑬ stands farther up Government Avenue, on your left, and opposite it on your right are the **SOUTH AFRICAN MUSEUM** ⑭ and the Planetarium. The temple in front of the South African Museum is the **DELVILLE**

WOOD MONUMENT ⑮. Walk through the alleyway on the left of the gallery onto Hatfield Street to reach the **SOUTH AFRICAN JEWISH MUSEUM** ⑯, the Cape Town Holocaust Center, and the imposing **GREAT SYNAGOGUE** ⑰, South Africa's mother synagogue. Carry on up Hatfield toward the mountain and take the first small tree-lined lane to the right; this will lead you back to Government Avenue. Turn left to go to **BERTRAM HOUSE** ⑱, at the top of the avenue, and then backtrack and turn left to cut across the front of the South African Museum to Queen Victoria Street. For something completely different, head down Bloem to **LONG STREET** ⑲. Turn left on Wale Street and walk four blocks to the **BO-KAAP** ⑳. Near the corner of Wale and Rose streets stands the **BO-KAAP MUSEUM** ㉑. Retrace your steps down Wale Street to **ST. GEORGE'S CATHEDRAL** ㉒. Across Wale is the entrance to **ST. GEORGE'S MALL** ㉓. From there turn left onto **CHURCH STREET** ㉔, with art galleries, African curio shops, a flea market, and a great coffee shop (Mozart's) between Burg and Long. If you have the time and energy, turn left onto Long to see the attractive old buildings; if not, turn right onto Longmarket and then amble around **GREENMARKET SQUARE** ㉕, the center of the city since 1710. The **OLD TOWN HOUSE** ㉖ faces the square on the mountain side. Work your way back to Long Street and walk away from the mountain. When you reach Strand Street, turn right to reach the **KOOPMANS–DE WET HOUSE** ㉗. Turn right again onto Burg, and you'll be back at Cape Town Tourism.

TIMING

To get the most from this tour, you'll need to set aside a whole day. Start at about 9, when most workers have finished their commute, and then stop for a long, leisurely lunch during the hottest part of the day, finishing the tour at about 4. Try to finish before 5, when rush hour congestion takes over the streets.

exploring cape town

WATERFRONT
Victoria Basin
Penny
Ferry
Victoria & Alfred
Waterfront Info Centre
Clocktower
Museum
South Arm
South Arm
Duncan
Dock
Robben
Island
0   500 yards
0   500 meters
Alfred
Basin
West Quay
Two Oceans Aquarium
S. A. Maritime
Museum
FORESHORE
Dock
Duncan
N1
Coen Steytler
CENTRAL
Heerengracht
D. F. Malan
Jan Smuts
Hertzog Boulevard
Civic
Center
Old Marine
Oswald Pirow
TO SEA
← POINT
M61 Main
Somerset
Prestwich
Chiappini
Long St. Loop
Riebeek
Adderley St.
Strand
2
Waterkant
Waterkant
3
General
Post Office
4
Strand
Castle St.
Hout
27 1
Burg St.
23
Darling St.
5
M4
Canterbury
Longmarket
25
Longmarket
7
Corporation
6
Caledon
Church
20
24
26
8
Albertus
Barrack
District
Six
Museum
Chiappini
Rose
Dorp
21
Dorp
19
22
9
Commercial
SCHOTSCHE
KLOOF
10
Roeland
Upper Leeuwen
11
Parliament St.
Long St. Loop
Signal Hill
Pentz
Upper Bloem
Bree
Queen Victoria St.
Government Ave.
12
St. John's St.
Hope
Buitenkant
Wesley
Military
Lion
Bryant
Loop
Kloof
Orange St.
13
16
17
Hatfield
Table
Mountain
15
14
18
Rheed
Park

Adderley Street, 2	City Hall, 6	Koopmans-De Wet House, 27	South African Library, 10
Bertram House, 18	Company's Gardens, 11	Long Street, 19	South African Museum, 14
Bo-Kaap, 20	Delville Wood Monument, 15	Old Town House, 26	South African National Gallery, 13
Bo-Kaap Museum, 21	Golden Acre, 3	Slave Tree, 8	
Cape Town Tourism Information Office, 1	Grand Parade, 5	South African Cultural History Museum, 9	St. George's Cathedral, 22
	Great Synagogue, 17		St. George's Mall, 23
Castle of Good Hope, 4	Greenmarket Square, 25	South African Jewish Museum, 16	Tuynhuys, 12
Church Street, 24	Groote Kerk, 7		

Sights to See

② **ADDERLEY STREET.** Originally named Heerengracht after a canal that ran the length of the avenue, this street has always been Cape Town's principal thoroughfare. It was once the favored address of the city's leading families, and its oak-shaded sidewalks served as a promenade for those who wanted to see and be seen. By the mid-19th century the oaks had all been chopped down and the canal covered as Adderley Street became the main commercial street. By 1908 it had become such a busy thoroughfare that the city fathers paved it with wooden blocks in an attempt to dampen the noise of countless wagons, carts, and hooves.

⑱ **BERTRAM HOUSE.** Built around 1840, this is the only surviving Georgian brick town house in Cape Town. Once a common sight in the city, these boxlike two-story houses were a response by the English community to Cape Dutch architecture. The projecting front porch was intended to shield the house from the worst effects of the frequent southeasters. The collection of furniture, silver, jewelry, and porcelain recaptures the look and feel of an early 19th-century home. The catalog available at the entrance describes the entire collection. *Government Ave. and Orange St., tel. 021/424–9381. R5. Tues.–Sat. 9:30–4:30.*

NEED A BREAK?
Government Avenue ends opposite the impressive gateway to the **MOUNT NELSON** hotel (76 Orange St., tel. 021/423–1000), complete with two pith-helmeted gatekeepers, which was erected in 1899 to welcome the Prince of Wales on his visit to the Cape. The Nellie, as it's known, remains Cape Town's most fashionable and genteel social venue. More important, it serves the city's best high tea, although the Table Bay Hotel at the V&A Waterfront also provides a memorable version. Both hotels provide a pastry selection to tempt even the most jaded palate.

★ ⑳ **BO-KAAP.** In the late 17th and early 18th centuries this district was the historic home of the city's Muslim population brought from the East as slaves. Today the area remains strongly Muslim, and it's fascinating to wander the narrow cobbled lanes past mosques and colorful flat-roof houses. Many homes combine elements of Cape Dutch and British architecture, and altogether they represent the largest collection of pre-1840 architecture in South Africa. The Bo-Kaap is also known as the Malay quarter, despite that its inhabitants originated from all over, including the Indonesian archipelago, India, Turkey, and Madagascar.

㉑ BO-KAAP MUSEUM. Built in the 18th century, this museum was originally the home of Abu Bakr Effendi, a well-known member of the Muslim community. The house has been furnished to re-create the lifestyle of a typical Malay family in the 19th century. Since the exhibits aren't labeled, you might do better to visit the museum as part of a guided tour of the Malay quarter. *71 Wale St., tel. 021/ 424–3846, www.museums.org.za. R5. Mon.–Sat. 9:30–4:30.*

❶ CAPE TOWN TOURISM INFORMATION OFFICE. This is one of the best information offices in South Africa. It's light and bright and breezy and filled with really helpful people. There is a *bureau de change*, a wine shop with tastings, an Internet café, coffee shop, and loads of information, including a National Parks desk, and an accommodations desk. *The Pinnacle at Burg and Castle Sts. (Box 1403), 8000, tel. 021/426–4260, fax 021/426–4263, www. cape-town.org. Weekdays 9–6, Sat. 8:30–2, Sun. 9–1.*

★ ❹ CASTLE OF GOOD HOPE. Far from a fairy-tale fantasy perched on a cliff, the Castle of Good Hope is a squat fortress that hunkers into the ground as if to avoid shell fire. Built between 1665 and 1676 by the Dutch East India Company (VOC) to replace an earthen fort constructed by Jan van Riebeeck in 1652, it's the oldest building in the country. Its pentagonal plan, with a diamond-shape bastion at each corner, is typical of the Old Netherlands defense system adopted in the early 17th century. The design was intended to allow covering fire to be provided for every portion of the castle. As added protection, the whole fortification was surrounded by a moat, with the sea nearly washing up against its walls. The castle served as both the VOC headquarters and the official governor's residence and still houses the regional headquarters of the National Defence Force. Despite its bellicose origins, no shot has ever been fired from its ramparts, except ceremonially.

You can wander around on your own or join a free guided tour at 11, noon, or 2. The excellent William Fehr Collection, in the governor's residence, consists of antiques, artifacts, and paintings of early Cape Town and South African history. Upstairs, John Thomas Baine's *The Greatest Hunt in Africa* celebrates a "hunt" in honor of Prince Alfred, when nearly 30,000 animals were driven together and slaughtered. *Buitenkant St., tel. 021/469–1249. R15. Mid-Jan.–mid-Dec., Mon.– Sun. 9–4:30; mid-Dec.–mid-Jan., daily 9–4.*

NEED A BREAK?
DE GOEWERNEUR RESTAURANT (Buitekant St., tel. 021/469– 1202) is in the central courtyard of the Castle of Good Hope and, from the veranda, has a pleasant view of the lawn and the buildings beyond. It is open Mon.–Sat. 9–4 for light meals and teas.

㉔ CHURCH STREET. The center of Cape Town's art and antiques business, the section between Burg and Long streets is a pedestrian mall, filled with art galleries, antiques dealers, and small cafés. This is the site of a daily antiques and flea market.

❻ CITY HALL. The old seat of local administration is home to the Cape Town Philharmonic Orchestra (which also holds performances at the Artscape Theatre Complex) and the City Library. It was from a balcony here, overlooking Darling Street, that Nelson Mandela gave his historic speech on his release from prison.

★ **⓫ COMPANY'S GARDENS.** In April 1652, a 43-acre garden was laid out by Jan van Riebeeck to supply fresh vegetables to ships on their way to the Dutch East Indies. By 1700 free burghers were

If You Can't Beat 'Em...

The following is a list of Cape Town festivals and events.

MID DEC.: The **Mother City Queer Project** is a costume party for the less conservative of Cape Town's residents, gay or straight. There's a different theme every year, but it's always as camp as a row of pink tents.

DEC.–FEB.: The **Spier Summer Season** is an extravaganza of music and theater performances at the Spier Estate, in Stellenbosch.

EARLY JAN.: The 17-day **Cape Coon Carnival** celebrates the New Year in grand style, as thousands of coloreds (the South African term for people of mixed Khoi-San, Malay, black, and/or European descent) dressed in bright costumes take to the streets of Cape Town to sing and dance.

EARLY MAR.: The **Argus Cycle Tour** is the largest individually timed race in the world, with about 40,000 competitors riding a scenic 115-km (about 70-mi) course.

LATE MAR.: The **North Sea Jazz Festival,** a showcase of international jazz, is held at Cape Town's Good Hope Centre.

MAR. OR APR.: The annual **Nederburg Auction** is the event on the wine calendar. It's the place to be seen, even if you don't bid, as South Africa's finest old and new wines go under the hammer.

APR.: The **Two Oceans Marathon** draws 8,000 runners for perhaps the most scenic race in the world, a grueling 56-km (35-mi) course that circumnavigates part of the Cape Peninsula.

AUG.–NOV.: The annual **whale migration** of southern right whales takes place along the coast from Port Elizabeth to Cape Town and beyond. In Cape Town they come very close to shore.

cultivating plenty of crops on their own land, and in time the VOC vegetable patch was transformed into a botanic garden. It remains a delightful haven in the city center, graced by fountains, exotic trees, rose gardens, aviaries, and a pleasant outdoor café. Close to Government Avenue, look for an **old well** that used to provide water for the town's residents and the garden. The old water pump, engraved with the maker's name and the date 1842, has been overtaken by an oak tree and now juts out of the tree's trunk some 6 ft above the ground. A huge **statue of Cecil Rhodes** looms over the path that runs through the center of the gardens. He points to the north, and an inscription reads, YOUR HINTERLAND IS THERE, a reference to Rhodes's dream of extending the British Empire from the Cape to Cairo. *Rhodes Dr., just past the university. Daily sunrise–sunset.*

⑮ DELVILLE WOOD MONUMENT. The monument honors South Africans who died in the fight for Delville Wood during the great Somme offensive of 1916. Of the 121 officers and 3,032 soldiers who participated in the three-day battle, only five officers and 750 soldiers survived unhurt. Facing the memorial is a **statue of Brigadier-General Lukin,** who commanded the South African infantry brigade during World War I.

③ GOLDEN ACRE. Until earlier in the century this part of the city was all at sea—literally. The land was reclaimed as part of a program to expand the docks. If you look at old paintings of the city, you will see that originally waves lapped at the very walls of the castle, now more than half a mile from the ocean. At the bottom of the escalator leading from the railway station into the Golden Acre is a thin black line that marks the approximate position of the shoreline in 1693. A bit farther on, enclosed in glass, are the remains of Cape Town's first reservoir, which was uncovered when the foundations of the Golden Acre were being dug.

⑤ GRAND PARADE. A statue of Edward VII serves as a parking attendant in this former parade ground, now a parking lot. It was here, after 27 years in prison, that Nelson Mandela addressed an adoring crowd of more than 100,000 supporters on his release on February 11, 1990. On Wednesday and Saturday mornings, this is the site of South Africa's oldest flea market. It's the best place to see some of the "real" Cape Town; many locals in the know get all manner of goods at bargain prices here. Pop into one of the kitschy food stalls and try a *gatsby* (a sandwich on a long roll filled with french fries, lettuce, tomato, and a choice of fresh or pickled fish, curry, or steak) or a *salomie* (roti wrapped around a curry filling) for a cheap lunch. Finish off with some *koeksusters* (sweet, braided, lightly spiced, deep-fried pastries) for dessert.

⓱ GREAT SYNAGOGUE. Built in 1903 in the baroque style, this synagogue has notable twin towers and a dome. This forms the center of a Jewish complex, which includes the South African Jewish Museum, the Jacob Gitlin Library, and the Cape Town Holocaust Centre, which is housed in the Albow Centre, next door. 88 Hatfield St., tel. 021/465–1405. Mon. 11–5, Tues. and Sun. 10–4, Wed. 11–3, Thurs. 10–3.

★ ⓼ GREENMARKET SQUARE. For more than a century this cobbled square served as a forum for public announcements, including the 1834 declaration abolishing slavery. In the 19th century the square became a vegetable market as well as a popular watering hole—the city's hardest boozers used to drink themselves comatose at the nearby Old Thatched Tavern and London Hotel. Today the square is a fun open-air market, with vendors selling a wide selection of clothing and sandals, as well as African jewelry, art, and fabrics. For gift buying it's virtually unbeatable.

⓻ GROOTE KERK (Great Church). One of the most famous churches in South Africa, Groote Kerk was built in 1841 on the site of an earlier Dutch Reformed church dating from 1704. The adjoining clock tower is all that remains of that earlier building. The enclosed pews, each with its own door, were owned by prominent families who could lock the door and avoid praying with the unwashed masses. The enormous pulpit is the work of sculptor Anton Anreith and carpenter Jan Jacob Graaff. The lions supporting it are carved from local stinkwood; the upper portion is Burmese teak. The organ, with nearly 6,000 pipes, is the largest in the southern hemisphere. Approximately 200 people are buried beneath the Batavian soapstone floor, including eight governors. There are free guided tours on request. *43 Adderley St. (enter on Church Sq.), tel. 021/461–7044. Free. Weekdays 10–2; services Sun. at 10 AM and 7 PM.*

㉗ **KOOPMANS–DE WET HOUSE.** Now a museum, this former 18th-century home is a haven of peace in the city center. The structure you see today dates largely from 1771 to 1793. Its neoclassic facade has been attributed to both Anton Anreith and Louis Thibault. The house enjoyed its heyday under Maria de Wet (1834–1906), a Cape Town socialite who entertained most of the major figures in Cape society, including Boer presidents and British governors. The furnishings date to the early 19th century, when the house belonged to Maria's grandmother. The collection includes stunning antiques, carpets, paintings, and porcelain. It's worth buying the printed guide to the museum, which describes every item in the collection. *35 Strand St., tel. 021/424–2473. R5. Tues.–Sat. 9:30–4:30.*

⑲ **LONG STREET.** The section of Long between Orange and Wale streets is lined with magnificently restored Georgian and Victorian buildings. Wrought-iron balconies and fancy curlicues on these colorful houses create an impression reminiscent of the French Quarter in New Orleans. During the 1960s Long Street did a good imitation of the Big Easy, including having a host of bars, prostitutes, and sleazy hotels. Today antiques dealers, secondhand bookstores (Clarke's is a must), pawnshops, the Pan-African Market, and funky and vintage clothing outlets make it the best browsing street in the city. There's also a good selection of backpackers' lodges. At the mountain end is Long Street Baths, an indoor swimming pool and old Turkish hammam.

㉖ **OLD TOWN HOUSE.** For 150 years this was the most important civic building in Cape Town. Built in 1755 as a guardhouse, it was also a meeting place for the burgher senate, a police station, and, from 1840 to 1905, Cape Town's city hall. The building is a beautiful example of urban Cape Dutch architecture, with thick whitewashed walls, green-and-white shutters, and small-paned windows. Today the former city hall is home to the Michaelis Collection, an extensive selection of 17th-century Dutch paintings, as well as changing exhibits. *Greenmarket Sq., tel. 021/424–6367, www. museumsonline.co.za. Free. Weekdays 10–5, Sat. 10–4.*

NEED A BREAK? The **IVY GARDEN** (Greenmarket Sq., tel. 021/424–6367), in the courtyard of the Old Town House, serves light lunches and teas in a leafy, green setting. Seating on the veranda overlooks the hustle and bustle of Greenmarket Square.

8 SLAVE TREE. Slaves were auctioned under the tree that once stood here. A cross section of the enormous Canadian pine is displayed at the South African Cultural History Museum. Slavery began in the Cape Colony in 1658, when free burghers petitioned the government for farmhands. The first group of 400 slaves arrived from Guinea, Angola, Batavia (modern Java), and Madagascar. During the first British occupation of the Cape (1795–1803), 17,000 slaves were brought from India, Ceylon, and the Philippines, swelling the total slave population to 30,000. Slavery was abolished by the British in 1834, an act that served as the final impetus for one of South Africa's great historical events, the Great Trek, when thousands of outraged Afrikaners set off in their covered wagons to establish a new state in the hinterland where they would be free from British taxation and laws.

★ **9 SOUTH AFRICAN CULTURAL HISTORY MUSEUM** (also known as the Slave Lodge). Built in 1679 by the Dutch East India Company to house slaves, this building, although beautiful, has a rather nasty history. Currently, the museum offers an excellent overview of South Africa's early settler history. Displays detailing the settlement and colonization of the Cape are superb; letters, coins, paintings, clothes, and furniture bring the period almost palpably to life. The museum also has minor collections of Roman, Greek, Egyptian, and Asian antiquities, as well as displays of antique silver, musical instruments, glass, ceramics, weapons, and coins. From 1815 to 1914 the building housed the supreme court. At the time of writing, the future of the museum was under debate, and it may soon be turned into a slavery museum. *Adderley and Wale Sts., tel. 021/461–8280, www.museums.org.za. R7. Mon.–Sat. 9:30–4:30.*

⑯ SOUTH AFRICAN JEWISH MUSEUM. The museum captures the story of South African Jewry from its early beginnings, spanning 150 years. The "Themes of Memories" (immigrant experiences), "Reality" (integration into South Africa), and "Dreams" (visions) exhibits are dynamically portrayed, represented by high-tech multimedia and interactive displays, reconstructed sets, models, and Judaica artifacts. There is also a computerized Discovery Center with a roots bank, a temporary gallery for changing exhibits, a museum restaurant and shop, and an auditorium. *88 Hatfield St., tel. 021/465–1546, www.sajewishmuseum.co.za. R25–R30. Sun.–Thurs. 10–5, Fri. 10–2.*

⑩ SOUTH AFRICAN LIBRARY. The National Reference Library, as it is also known, owes its existence to Lord Charles Somerset, governor of the Cape Colony, who in 1818 imposed a wine tax to fund the creation of a library that would "place the means of knowledge within the reach of the youth of this remote corner of the Globe." In 1860 the library moved into its current home, a neoclassic building modeled after the Fitzwilliam Museum in Cambridge, England. The extensive collection of Africana includes the works of many 18th- and 19th-century explorers. *Botanical Gardens, tel. 021/424–6320. Free. Weekdays 9–5.*

⑭ SOUTH AFRICAN MUSEUM. This is a natural history museum with some interesting cultural hangovers. Probably the strangest is the section on ethnography and archaeology, which, many argue, should be in the Cultural History Museum. Far more interesting is the section on the fossil remains of prehistoric reptiles and other animals, and the quite spectacular Whale Well—where musical recitals are often held, under suspended life-size casts of enormous marine mammals. The adjoining planetarium stages a variety of shows throughout the week. *25 Queen Victoria St., tel. 021/424–3330, fax 021/424–6716, www.museums.org.za. Museum R8, planetarium R10. Museum daily 10–5; planetarium shows Tues.–Fri. at 1, weekends at noon, 1, and 2:30.*

★ ⑬ **SOUTH AFRICAN NATIONAL GALLERY.** Don't miss this art gallery. The museum houses a good collection of 19th- and 20th-century European and British works, but it's most interesting for its South African works, many of which reflect the country's traumatic history. The director is known for innovative, brave, and sometimes controversial exhibitions. The museum café serves salads, sandwiches, pastas, and cakes. Free guided tours are given on Wednesday at 1 and Saturday at 3. *Government Ave., Gardens, tel. 021/465–1628, www.museums.org.za. R5. Tues.–Sun. 10–5.*

㉒ **ST. GEORGE'S CATHEDRAL.** The church was once the religious seat of Archbishop Desmond Tutu, who, in his position as the first black archbishop of Cape Town, vociferously denounced apartheid and relentlessly pressed for a democratic government. The Anglican cathedral was designed by Sir Herbert Baker in the Gothic Revival style; construction began in 1901, using sandstone from Table Mountain. The structure has the largest stained-glass window in the country, some beautiful examples of late-Victorian stained glass, and a 1,000-year-old Coptic cross. If you want to hear the magnificent organ, go to the choral evensong at 5:30 on Wednesday evening, the 9:15 AM or 7 PM mass on Sunday, or the 11 AM mass on the last Sunday of every month. *Wale St., tel. 021/424–7360. Free. Daily 8–5. Services weekdays at 7:15 and 1:15; Tues. and Fri. at 5:30 PM; Sat. at 8 AM; Sun. at 7 AM, 8 AM, 9:15 AM, and 7 PM.*

㉓ **ST. GEORGE'S MALL.** This promenade stretches almost all the way to the Foreshore. Shops and cafés line the mall, and street vendors hawk everything from T-shirts to African arts and crafts. Buskers and dancers gather daily to entertain the crowds.

⑫ **TUYNHUYS (TOWN HOUSE).** Parts of the Tuynhuys date to the late 17th and early 18th centuries. The building contains the offices of the state president and is not open to the public.

THE VICTORIA & ALFRED WATERFRONT

The Victoria & Alfred Waterfront is the culmination of a long-term project undertaken to breathe new life into the historical dockland of the city. It is one of Cape Town's most vibrant and exciting attractions and is the focus of the city's nightlife and entertainment scene. Hundreds of shops, movie theaters, restaurants, and bars share quarters in restored warehouses and dock buildings, all connected by pedestrian plazas and promenades. It's clean, it's safe, and it's car free.

Sights to See

AGFA AMPHITHEATRE. This popular outdoor performance space mounts shows almost daily, ranging from concerts by the Cape Town Philharmonic Orchestra to gigs by jazz and rock bands. Check with the Victoria and Albert Information Centre for the schedule of events. The amphitheater stands on the site where, in 1860, teenage Prince Alfred inaugurated the construction of a breakwater to protect shipping in the harbor. Table Bay was never an ideal natural harbor. In winter devastating northwesterly winds pounded ships caught in the exposed waters. Between 1647 and 1870 more than 190 ships went down in Table Bay. Since the breakwater was built, only 40 ships have foundered here.

FERRYMAN'S TAVERN. With the heady smell of malt emanating from **Mitchell's Brewery** adjoining the pub, you won't have to wait long for a nice cool one. Constructed in 1877 of bluestone and Table Mountain sandstone, this is one of the oldest buildings in the harbor. Before 1912 the temperance movement in Cape Town had managed to force a ban on the sale of alcohol within the docks. As a result, a host of pubs sprang up just outside the dock gates, particularly along Dock Road. *Market Plaza, tel. 021/419–7748.*

HARBOUR MASTER'S RESIDENCE. Built in 1860, this edifice has a beautiful, century-old dragon tree, a native of the Canary Islands, in front. The resin of this tree species, called dragon's blood, was used in Europe to treat dysentery and is still used in all manner of Asian medicines.

MITCHELL'S WATERFRONT BREWERY. This is one of a handful of microbreweries in South Africa. The brewery produces four beers: Foresters Draught Lager, Bosuns Bitter, Ravenstout, and Ferryman's Ale. Tours, for which reservations are essential, include beer tasting and a look at the fermentation tanks. *Dock Rd., tel. 021/418–2461. R10. Weekdays 11–3.*

★ **ROBBEN ISLAND.** Made famous by its most illustrious inhabitant, Nelson Rolihlahla Mandela, this island, whose name is Dutch for "seals," has a long and sad history. It has been a prison, leper colony, mental institution, and military base. Now, as a museum, it is finally filling a positive and empowering role. One of the first prisoners was Autshumato, known to the early Dutch settlers as "Harry the Hottentot." In 1820 the British thought they could solve some of their problems on the Eastern Cape frontier by banishing Xhosa leader Makhanda to the island. Both Autshumato and Makhanda (also spelled Makana) escaped by rowboat, but Makhanda didn't make it. Today, the sleek high-speed ferries to the island are called *Autshumato* and *Makana.*

The **Robben Island Museum** (tel. 021/419–1300; 021/419–1300 tours, www.robbenisland.org.za) organizes all tours. Guides are often former political prisoners. Other operators that advertise Robben Island tours just take you on a boat trip. Tours leave from the jetty near the Fish Quay ("Berties") on the hour every hour from 9 to 12 and 2 to 3. The last boat leaves the island at 6. The boat crossing takes 30 minutes. The island tour itself lasts

2½ hours, during which time you walk through the prison and see the cell in which Mandela was imprisoned, as well as the stark quarry where the former president pounded rocks for so many years. Reserve in advance during peak season (mid-December to mid-January). Tours are R100.

SOUTH AFRICAN MARITIME MUSEUM. The museum provides a look at ships and the history of Table Bay, including a model of Cape Town Harbor as it appeared in 1886. In the model workshop you can watch modelers build scale replicas of famous ships. Also here is the **SAS *Somerset,*** the only surviving boom-defense vessel in the world. During World War II harbors were protected against enemy submarines and divers by booms, essentially metal mesh curtains drawn across the harbor entrance. The *Somerset* (then named the HMS *Barcross*) controlled the boom across Saldanha Bay, north of Cape Town. You can explore the entire ship, including the bridge and the engine room. *Dock Rd., tel. 021/419–2505. R10, SAS Somerset R5. Daily 10–5.*

TIME BALL TOWER. The tower was built in 1894, before the advent of modern navigational equipment, when ships' crews needed to know the exact time to help them calculate longitude. Navigators set their clocks by the time ball, which fell every day at 1 PM, much like the ball that marks the stroke of midnight in New York's Times Square on New Year's Eve.

★ ♻ **TWO OCEANS AQUARIUM.** Possibly one of the finest aquariums in the world, Two Oceans has stunning displays of marine life in the warm Indian Ocean and the cold Atlantic Ocean. There's a touch pool for children and opportunities for certified divers to explore the vast, five-story kelp forest or the predator tank, where you share the water with a couple of large ragged-tooth sharks (*Carcharias taurus*). You can even do a copper helmet dive with antique dive equipment in the predator tank. The aquarium runs a baby-sitting service where you drop your children (ages 7–12) off anytime after 6:30 PM with a sleeping bag, and head off to the waterfront to party (R85 per child). Kids get a meal, a gift pack, a tour, are shown a video, play games, and sleep surrounded by fish. There is full-time supervision, and security is tight. You may pick them up after midnight if you prefer. *Dock Rd., Waterfront, tel. 021/418–3823, www.aquarium.co.za. R45–R55; R350 for dives (R275 with own gear); R950 for copper-helmet dive. Daily 9:30–6.*

UNION-CASTLE HOUSE. Designed in 1919 by Sir Herbert Baker, the house was headquarters for the famous Union-Castle shipping line. Before World War II many English-speaking South Africans considered England home, even if they had never been there. Mail steamers, carrying both mail and passengers, sailed weekly between South Africa and England. In 1977, amid much pomp and ceremony, the last Union-Castle mail ship, the *Windsor Castle*, made its final passage to England. Even today older South Africans like to wax lyrical about the joys of a voyage on one of those steamers. Union-Castle House is now home to several banks and small businesses. Inside Standard Bank you can still see the iron rings in the ceiling from which mailbags were hung. *Quay 4.*

VICTORIA & ALFRED WATERFRONT INFORMATION CENTRE. The center, opposite the V&A Hotel, has the lowdown on everything happening in the area, including upcoming events and shows. Here you can arrange walking tours of the waterfront, book accommodations, and get information about the whole Western Cape. A scale model shows what the waterfront will look like when it's finished. *Pierhead, tel. 021/408–7600, fax 021/408–7605, www.waterfront.com. Oct.–Apr., daily 9–6; May–Sept., daily 8–5.*

VICTORIA BASIN. Constructed between 1870 and 1905, the basin was created to accommodate the huge increase in shipping following the discovery of diamonds at Kimberley and gold on the Witwatersrand. Across the basin is the South Arm, a debarkation point for British troops, horses, and material during the Boer War (1899–1902). Much of the fodder for the

Your checklist for a perfect journey

WAY AHEAD
- Devise a trip budget.
- Write down the five things you want most from this trip. Keep this list handy before and during your trip.
- Make plane or train reservations. Book lodging and rental cars.
- Arrange for pet care.
- Check your passport. Apply for a new one if necessary.
- Photocopy important documents and store in a safe place.

A MONTH BEFORE
- Make restaurant reservations and buy theater and concert tickets. Visit fodors.com for links to local events.
- Familiarize yourself with the local language or lingo.

TWO WEEKS BEFORE
- Replenish your supply of medications.
- Create your itinerary.
- Enjoy a book or movie set in your destination to get you in the mood.

- Develop a packing list. Shop for missing essentials. Repair and launder or dry-clean your clothes.

A WEEK BEFORE
- Stop newspaper deliveries. Pay bills.
- Acquire traveler's checks.
- Stock up on film.
- Label your luggage.
- Finalize your packing list— take less than you think you need.
- Create a toiletries kit filled with travel-size essentials.
- Get lots of sleep. Don't get sick before your trip.

A DAY BEFORE
- Drink plenty of water.
- Check your travel documents.
- Get packing!

DURING YOUR TRIP
- Keep a journal/scrapbook.
- Spend time with locals.
- Take time to explore. Don't plan too much.

British horses, shipped from Argentina, was catastrophically infested with rats and fleas. As a result, bubonic plague broke out in Cape Town in February 1901, creating panic in the city. African dockworkers, suspected of harboring the disease, were forbidden to leave the city and ultimately confined to specific quarters. During the epidemic 766 people contracted the plague; 371 died.

THE PENINSULA

This driving tour takes you south from Cape Town on a loop of the peninsula, heading through the scenic southern suburbs before running down the False Bay coast to Cape Point. It's a magnificent drive back to the city along the wild Atlantic coast.

Numbers in the text correspond to numbers in the margin and on the Cape Peninsula map.

A Good Drive

Take the N2 or De Waal Drive (M3) out of the city center. The two highways merge near Groote Schuur Hospital and split again soon after. Bear right, taking the M3 (signposted SOUTHERN SUBURBS/MUIZENBERG), and look up at the mountain to see zebras, gnu, and eland grazing. After 1 km (½ mi) you pass **MOSTERT'S MILL** ㉘ on your left, one of two remaining windmills in the Cape, and on your right is the campus of the University of Cape Town, nestled against the slopes of Devil's Peak. Continue on the M3 for another 1 km (½ mi) to the exit marked with a sign to the **RHODES MEMORIAL** ㉙. Return to the M3 and head south toward Muizenberg. After 1½ km (1 mi), exit right onto Rhodes Avenue (M63). This road winds through large trees to the **KIRSTENBOSCH NATIONAL BOTANIC GARDENS** ㉚, one of the most beautiful spots in the Cape. Turn right as you leave the botanic gardens. When you reach a T junction, turn right again and begin the winding climb to the pass at Constantia Nek. From the traffic circle at the top you can either cut over the mountains and down into Hout Bay or turn left onto the M41 (the sign reads WYNBERG AND GROOT CONSTANTIA) and begin the snaking descent into Constantia and **GROOT CONSTANTIA** ㉛. Leaving Groot Constantia, turn right on Main Road and then right again onto Ladies Mile Extension (a sign points you to Muizenberg and Bergvliet). Another right at the first traffic light puts you on Spaanschemat River Road, and a farther right turn funnels you onto Klein Constantia Road. Follow this to **BUITENVERWACHTING** ㉜. Turn left out of Buitenverwachting and continue for ½ km (¼ mi) to **KLEIN CONSTANTIA** ㉝.

Head back down Klein Constantia Road, and turn right into Spaanschemat River Road. After about 3 km (2 mi) turn left onto Tokai Road and right again at the PORTER SCHOOL sign and drive 1 km (½ mi) to **TOKAI MANOR** ㉞. Return to the junction and continue straight on Tokai Road, through the traffic circle, and to Steenberg Country Hotel, Golf Estate, and Vineyards on your right. On the left is Pollsmoor Prison, where Nelson Mandela stayed after he was moved from Robben Island. Turn left at the T junction and continue to the Main Road (M4) and turn right again. After ½ km (¼ mi) Boyes Drive leads off the M4. The M4, or Main Road, on the other hand, takes you through **MUIZENBERG** ㉟, where the Main Road runs parallel to the sea. Watch on your right for a De Post Huys, a small thatched building with rough whitewashed walls, and the imposing facade of the Natale Labia Museum. Continue to Rhodes Cottage Museum. From Muizenberg Main Road heads down the peninsula, hugging the shore of False Bay. Strung along this coastline are a collection of small villages that long ago merged to form a thin suburban belt between the ocean and the mountains. **KALK BAY** ㊱, **FISH HOEK** ㊲, and **SIMONSTOWN** ㊳ are all on this stretch. Simonstown is the last community of any size before you reach Cape Point. From here the road traverses a wild, windswept landscape as beautiful as it is desolate. You can stop at tiny **BOULDERS BEACH** ㊴ to look at the colony of African penguins. The mountains, covered with rugged fynbos, descend almost straight into the sea. Don't be surprised to see troops of baboons lounging beside the road as you approach the **CAPE OF GOOD HOPE** ④ section of Cape Peninsula National Park. Close the windows of your car and don't attempt to feed the baboons. They are dangerous. Before you reach the Cape Point gate, look left to see the beautiful settlement of Smitswinkel Bay—accessible only on foot via a steep and narrow path. Turn left out of the Cape Point gate onto the M65 to **SCARBOROUGH** ④ and **KOMMETJIE** ④.

From Kommetjie the M65 leads to a major intersection. Turn left onto the M6 (Hout Bay), go through one set of lights, and then turn left again, following the signs to Hout Bay. The road passes through the small community of **NOORDHOEK** ④ before beginning its treacherous climb around **CHAPMAN'S PEAK DRIVE** ④, which has been closed indefinitely because of dangerous rock falls. So go and have a look at Noordhoek, and then retrace your route to the beginning of **OU KAAPSE WEG** ④, Old Cape Road. Head over the mountain through the Silvermine section of the CPNP, and turn left at the T junction. Continue past Steenberg and Pollsmoor, and then turn left into Klein Constantia Road as if you were returning to Buitenverwachting, but turn immediately right. Continue to the end, turn right into Pagasvlei Road, follow the curve, and then turn left into Constantia Main Road. You'll go past Groot Constantia on your left. Stay left at the traffic circle at Constantia Nek and drive down into **HOUT BAY** ④. Turn right onto the M6 (a sign reads CITY AND LLANDUDNO). After less than than 1 km (½ mi), turn right on Valley Road to the **WORLD OF BIRDS** ④. From Hout Bay the M6 climbs past the exclusive community of Llandudno and then runs along the coast to **CAMPS BAY** ④. Follow Victoria Road (M6) out of Camps Bay and turn right at the sign reading KLOOF NEK ROUND HOUSE. This road snakes up the mountain to a five-way intersection at Kloof Nek. Make a sharp left onto the road leading to **SIGNAL HILL** ④. For more great views of the city, return to the Kloof Nek intersection and take **TAFELBERG ROAD** ⑤.

the cape peninsula

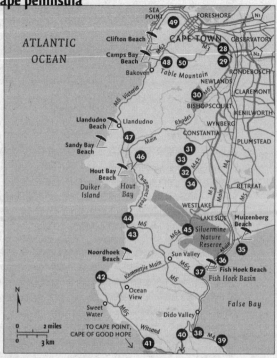

Boulders Beach, 39

Buitenverwachting, 32

Camps Bay, 48

Cape of Good Hope, 40

Chapman's Peak Drive, 44

Fish Hoek, 37

Groot Constantia, 31

Hout Bay, 46

Kalk Bay, 36

Kirstenbosch National Botanic Gardens, 30

Klein Constantia, 33

Kommetjie, 42

Mostert's Mill, 28

Muizenberg, 35

Noordhoek, 43

Ou Kaapse Weg, 45

Rhodes Memorial, 29

Scarborough, 41

Signal Hill, 49

Simonstown, 38

Tafelberg Road, 50

Tokai Manor, 34

World of Birds, 47

TIMING

You could spend three days on this tour, either moving slowly around the peninsula, staying in a different guest house each night, or scuttling back to a central spot at the end of the day. The distances are not great, and you could easily base yourself in the southern suburbs and head out in a different direction on each of two or three days. Or pick a few things that interest you most and spend a single day just visiting those spots.

Sights to See

★ **39** **BOULDERS BEACH.** This series of small coves lies on the outskirts of Simonstown among giant boulders. Part of the Cape Peninsula National Park, the beach is best known for its resident colony of African penguins. You must stay out of the fenced-off breeding beach, but the birds will probably come waddling up to you to take a look. *www.cpnp.co.za*. R10. Daily 9–6.

BOYES DRIVE. If you prefer scenic views to historical sites, Boyes Drive is probably a better option than the main highway. The drive runs high along the mountains, offering panoramic views of False Bay and the Hottentots Holland Mountains before rejoining the M4 at Kalk Bay.

32 **BUITENVERWACHTING.** A gorgeous winery that was also once part of Van der Stel's original Constantia farm, Buitenverwachting means "beyond expectation," and its setting certainly surpasses anything you might have imagined: An oak-lined avenue leads past the Cape Dutch homestead to the thatched modern cellar. Acres of vines spread up hillsides flanked by more towering oaks and the rocky crags of the Constantiaberg.

Buitenverwachting's wine is just as superb as its setting. The largest seller is the slightly dry buiten blanc, an easy-drinking blend of a few varieties. The best red is Christine, which until the 1991 vintage was known as Grand Vin; it's a blend of mostly cabernet sauvignon and 30% merlot. The winery's restaurant is probably the finest in the Cape. *Off Klein Constantia Rd., tel. 021/794–5190, fax 021/794–1351. Tastings free. Weekdays 9–5, Sat. 9–1.*

NEED A
BREAK? Buitenverwachting serves great picnic lunches under the oaks on the estate's lawns. It's an idyllic setting and a most civilized way to cap a morning of wine tasting. Each picnic basket is packed with a selection of breads, meat, chicken, pâtés, and cheeses. You can buy a bottle of estate wine as an accompaniment to the meal. The **PICNIC** costs R55 per person, and reservations are essential. *tel. 021/794–1012. Closed Sun.*

㊽ CAMPS BAY. This is a popular holiday resort with a long beach and plenty of restaurants and bars. The craggy faces of the Twelve Apostles, huge granite buttresses reaching down to the sea from the mountains behind, loom over the town.

★ **㊵ CAPE OF GOOD HOPE PARK.** Part of Cape Peninsula National Park, this area covers some 19,100 acres. Much of the park consists of rolling hills covered with fynbos and laced with miles of walking trails; maps are available at the park entrance. It also has beautiful deserted beaches. Eland, baboon, ostrich, and bontebok are among the animals that roam the park. A tarred road runs 14 km (8 mi) to the tip of the peninsula. A turnoff leads to the rocky Cape of Good Hope, the southwesternmost point of the continent; a plaque marks the spot. No plaque is needed at Cape Point, where a dramatic knife's edge of rock slices into the Atlantic. Looking out to sea from the viewing platform, you feel you're at the southern tip of Africa, even though that honor officially belongs to Cape Agulhas, about 160 km (100 mi) to the southeast. From Cape Point the views of False Bay and the Hottentots Holland Mountains are breathtaking. The walk up to the viewing platform and the old lighthouse is very steep; a funicular (R22 round-trip, R15 one-way) makes the run every few minutes. Take a jacket or sweater—the wind can be cold. A large sit-down restaurant has better views than food, and a kiosk sells snacks. During peak season, visit Cape Point early in the day; otherwise you'll be swamped by horrendous numbers of tourists. The parks board books ecorted bike trips to the point and an overnight hike with basic accommodations and incredible views. Be warned that baboons in the parking lot have been known to steal food and can be dangerous if provoked. *Off the M65, tel. 021/780–9526 or 021/780–9204, www.cpnp.co.za. R20. Oct.–Mar., daily 7–6; Apr.–Sept., daily 7–5.*

44 CHAPMAN'S PEAK DRIVE. This fantastically scenic drive has been indefinitely closed due to deterioration and rock falls. However, you may drive onto the first section from Hout Bay just to get an idea of what it was like. With any luck it may be reopened in the future.

CONSTANTIA. Backed by the rugged mountains of the Constantiaberg and overlooking the Cape Flats and False Bay, Constantia is an idyllic spot to while away a day—or a week. Vineyards carpet the lower slopes, while plantations of pine predominate higher up. This is very much the domain of the suburban gentry. If you don't have time to visit the Winelands, Constantia is a must. Here you'll find five excellent estates— Buitenverwachting, Groot Constantia, Klein Constantia, Constantia Uitsig, and the relatively new Steenberg.

DE POST HUYS. One of the oldest buildings in the country, De Post Huys was constructed in 1673 as a lookout post and signal station. It now houses the **SA Police Historical Museum,** with exhibits ranging from drug-related paraphernalia to the role of the police in the freedom struggle. *Main Rd., tel. 021/788–7035 or 021/788–7031. Free. Weekdays 8–3:30.*

37 FISH HOEK. This is one of the most popular resort towns on the False Bay coast, with a smooth, sandy beach that is protected on the south side from the summer southeasters by Elsies Peak. It's one of the best places to see whales during calving season (August to November) though there have been whale sightings as early as June and as late as January. Until recently, Fish Hoek was the only teetotaling town in the country. In 1810 Lord Charles Somerset issued the first grant of British crown land in Fish Hoek on condition that no wine house should ever exist on the property. Somerset was evidently alarmed by the excesses associated with a wine house near Kommetjie, where wagon drivers would become too drunk to deliver their supplies to the Royal Navy at Simonstown. Jagers Walk, from the south side of Fish Hoek Beach to Sunny Cove, is a pleasant, scenic, wheelchair-friendly pathway that meanders through the rocks, giving access to some sheltered natural rock pools that are great for swimming. The snorkeling is good, too.

★ ③① **GROOT CONSTANTIA.** The town of Constantia takes its name from this wine estate, founded in 1685 by Simon van der Stel, one of the first Dutch governors of the Cape. After his death in 1712 the land was subdivided, with the heart of the estate preserved at Groot Constantia. The enormous complex is a national monument and is by far the most commercial and touristy of the wineries. Van der Stel's magnificent homestead, the oldest in the Cape, lies at the center of Groot Constantia. It's built in traditional Cape Dutch style, with thick whitewashed walls, a thatched roof, small-pane windows, and ornate gables. It is furnished with exquisite period pieces. The old wine cellar behind the manor house, built in 1791, is most famous for its own ornate gable, designed by sculptor Anton Anreith. In the cellar is a wine museum, with displays of antique wine-drinking and storage vessels.

In the 19th century the sweet wines of Groot Constantia were highly regarded in Europe and especially favored by King Louis Philippe and Bismarck. Today the estate is known for its splendid reds. The best is the Gouverneurs Reserve, made primarily from cabernet sauvignon grapes with smaller amounts of merlot and cabernet franc. The pinotage is consistently good, too; it reaches its velvety prime in about five years. The estate operates two restaurants: the elegant Jonkershuis (☞ Eating Out) and the Tavern, which serves light meals at picnic tables on the lawn. You can also pack a lunch and relax on the lawns behind the wine cellar. *Off Main Rd., tel. 021/ 794–5128 for winery; 021/794–5067 for museum. Museum R8, wine tasting R12, cellar tour R11. Museum: daily 10–5; winery: Dec.–Apr., daily 9:30–6; May–Nov., daily 10–5.*

GROOTE SCHUUR HOSPITAL. Dr. Christian Barnard performed the world's first heart transplant here in 1967. Just off Main Road you'll see this visible landmark on the slopes of Table Mountain below the scenic De Waal Drive. The Transplant Museum and Educational Center is worth a visit if you're interested in medical history or techniques. *tel. 021/404–5232. R5. Weekdays 9–2.*

③ HOUT BAY. Cradled in a lovely bay and guarded by a 1,000-ft peak known as the Sentinel, Hout Bay is the center of Cape Town's crayfishing industry, and the town operates several fish-processing plants. Mariner's Wharf is Hout Bay's salty answer to the waterfront in Cape Town, a collection of bars and restaurants on the quayside. You can buy fresh fish at a seafood market and take it outside to be grilled. You should also try *snoek*—a barracuda-like fish that is traditionally eaten smoked. Cruise boats depart from Hout Bay's harbor to view the **seal colony** on Duiker Island.

IRMA STERN MUSEUM. This museum is dedicated to the works and art collection of Stern (1894–1966), one of South Africa's greatest painters. The museum is administered by the University of Cape Town and occupies the Firs, the artist's home for 38 years. She is best known for African studies, particularly her paintings of indigenous people inspired by trips to the Congo and Zanzibar. Her collection of African artifacts, including priceless Congolese stools and carvings, is superb. *Cecil Rd., Rosebank, tel. 021/685–5686, www.museums.org.za/irma. R7. Tues.–Sat. 10–5.*

★ ③ KALK BAY. The name of Kalk Bay recalls that seashells were once baked in large kilns near the shore to produce lime (*kalk*). This is one of the most fascinating destinations on the peninsula. A small harbor, where you can buy fish so fresh it wriggles, shelters a weathered fishing fleet, and tiny cottages crowd the narrow cobbled streets, clinging to the mountain. Funky crafts shops, galleries, antiques shops, and cozy bistros can fill a whole day of rambling. Gnarled fishingfolk rub shoulders with Rastafarians, surfers, yuppies, New Age trendies, and genteel ladies with blue hair rinses. The Brass Bell is a great place to down a few beers in the sun while local surfers strut their stuff on Kalk Bay Reef—a nice hollow left—barely yards from your comfortable table. You can walk up one of the many steep stairways to Boyes Drive and from there up the mountain.

★ ③ **KIRSTENBOSCH NATIONAL BOTANIC GARDENS.** The gardens extend up the eastern slopes of Table Mountain, overlooking the Cape Flats and distant Hottentots Holland Mountains. Walking trails meander through the gardens, and grassy banks are ideal for a picnic or afternoon nap. The plantings are limited to species native to southern Africa, including fynbos—hardy, thin-leaved plants that proliferate in the Cape. Among these are proteas, including silver trees and king proteas, ericas, and *restios* (reeds). Highlights include a large cycad garden, the Bird Bath (a beautiful stone pool built around a crystal-clear spring), and the fragrance garden, which is wheelchair friendly and has a tapping rail and braille interpretive boards. Those who have difficulty walking can take a comprehensive tour lasting between 45 minutes and an hour (R12) by six-person cart. There is also a wheelchair trail that goes off the main paths into the wilder section of the park and gets close to the feel of the mountain walks. Concerts are held here on summer Sundays starting an hour before sunset. With Table Mountain as a magnificent backdrop and the gardens all around, you can catch the best of South Africa's entertainment with everything from classical music to township jazz to rock and roll. A visitor center leads into the conservatory and houses a restaurant, bookstore, and coffee shop. *Rhodes Ave., Newlands, tel. 021/799–8800, www.nbi.ac.za. R15. Apr.–Aug., daily 8–6; Sept.–Mar., daily 8–7.*

③③ KLEIN CONSTANTIA. Klein (rhymes with "stain") means "small" in Afrikaans and indicates the relative size of this portion of van der Stel's original Constantia estate. The winery has an impressive modern cellar, deliberately unobtrusive so as not to detract from the vine-covered mountain slopes. Its Cape Dutch homestead, visible as you drive in, was built in the late 18th century. This estate produces wines of superb quality, as awards displayed in the tasting area attest. The excellent sauvignon blanc is used as a point of reference by many South African connoisseurs and vintners. The closest you'll come to the famous Constantia wine of the 18th century is the Vin de Constance, a sweet wine made from predominantly Muscat de Frontignan grapes. The cabernet sauvignon is one of the best produced in the Cape—a collector's wine that develops wonderfully over time. *Klein Constantia Rd., Constantia, tel. 021/794–5188, fax 021/794–2464, www. kleinconstantia.com. Free. Weekdays 9–5, Sat. 9–1. Cellar tours by appointment. No tours on Sat.*

④② KOMMETJIE. A pleasant, somewhat isolated suburb, Kommetjie has a scenic 45-minute walk down Long Beach that leads to the wreck of the *Kakapo*, a steamship that ran aground on her maiden voyage in 1900. This is a surfer's paradise, with some really big wave spots and a few gentler breaks. The nearby Imhoffs Gift complex is a must, especially if you have children. There are a nature park, with loads of birds, a snake park, camel rides, horse rides, a petting farm, crafts shops and, of course, a coffee shop.

②⑧ MOSTERT'S MILL. Built in 1796, this thatched wheat mill consists of a tower with a rotating cap to which sails were attached. Mills like this were once common in the area. Inside is the original mechanism, but it's not necessarily worth pulling off the highway to see. *Rhodes Dr., Mowbray, no phone. Daily 9–5.*

③⑤ MUIZENBERG. At the turn of the 20th century this was the premier bathing resort in South Africa, attracting many of the country's wealthy mining magnates, as the many mansions along Baden

Powell Drive attest. Long gone, though, are the days when anyone thought of Muizenberg as chic. A drab complex of shops and fast-food outlets, complete with kiddie pools and miniature golf, blights the beachfront, and the views of mountains and sea cannot make up for it. The whole area is in a state of not-so-genteel decay, and many beautiful art deco beachfront buildings have become slums. That doesn't stop beginner surfers and keen dog walkers from utilizing the still-wonderful beach, but they give the area on the sea side of the railway line a miss.

43 NOORDHOEK. Noordhoek is a popular beach community with stunning white sands that stretch forever. The bordering village has become a retreat for the arts-and-crafts community, and there are lots of galleries and boutiques selling unusual items. You can walk all the way between Kommetjie and Noordhoek on the aptly named Long Beach. It's also very popular with horseback riders and surfers.

★ **45 OU KAAPSE WEG.** This is the shortest (and most scenic) route between Noordhoek and Constantia since the closure of Chapman's Peak. It's spectacular in its own right, with lovely flowers and distant vistas of False Bay, in the east, and the Atlantic, in the west.

RHODES COTTAGE MUSEUM. Considering the great power wielded by Cecil John Rhodes (1853–1902), one of Britain's great empire builders, his seaside cottage was surprisingly humble and spare. Yet this is where the man who was instrumental in the development of present-day South Africa chose to spend his last days in 1902, preferring the cool sea air of Muizenberg to the stifling opulence of his home at Groote Schuur. The cottage, including the bedroom where he died, has been completely restored. Other rooms display photos documenting Rhodes's life. His remains are buried in the Matopos Hills, in Zimbabwe. *246 Main Rd., Muizenberg, tel. 021/788–1816. Free. Tues.–Sun. 10–1 and 2–5.*

★ ㉙ **RHODES MEMORIAL.** Rhodes served as prime minister of the Cape from 1890 to 1896. He made his fortune in the diamond rush at Kimberley, but his greatest dream was to forge a Cape–Cairo railway, a tangible symbol of British dominion in Africa. The classical-style granite memorial sits high on the slopes of Devil's Peak, on part of Rhodes's old estate, Groote Schuur. A mounted rider symbolizing energy faces north toward the continent for which Rhodes felt such passion. A bust of Rhodes dominates the temple—ironically, he's leaning on one hand as if he's about to nod off. *Off Rhodes Dr., Rondebosch. Free.*

NEED A BREAK? The **RHODES MEMORIAL TEA GARDEN** (tel. 021/689–9151), tucked under towering pines behind the memorial, is a pleasant spot that serves tea or a light lunch.

㊶ **SCARBOROUGH.** The town is a tiny holiday community with one of the best beaches on the peninsula. Scarborough is becoming popular with artists and craftspeople, and you'll find their offerings exhibited at informal galleries. From Scarborough to Kommetjie the road hugs the shoreline, snaking between the mountains and the crashing surf. This part of the shore is considered unsafe for swimming, but experienced surfers and boardsailers revel in the wind and waves.

㊾ **SIGNAL HILL.** Here the road swings around the shoulder of Lion's Head, then runs along the flank of Signal Hill. The views of the city below and Table Mountain are superb. The road ends at a parking lot overlooking Sea Point and all of Table Bay. Be careful around here, especially if it's deserted. There have been incidents of violent crime.

★ ㊳ **SIMONSTOWN.** Because Simonstown is a naval base, and has been for many years, a large part of the seafront is out of bounds. Even worse, defense force personnel knock off at 4 during the week, when the single-lane road going out of Simonstown is stop–start traffic (as it is in the morning). Despite this it's an attractive town with many lovely old buildings and is close to what are possibly the peninsula's best swimming beaches, Seaforth and Boulders. Simonstown has had a long association with the Royal Navy. It was here in 1795 that British troops landed before defeating the Dutch at the Battle of Muizenberg, and the town served as a base for the Royal Navy from 1814 to 1957, when the naval base was handed over to the South African navy.

Jubilee Square, a dockside plaza that serves as the de facto town center, is just off the main road (St. George's Road). Next to the dock wall stands a sculpture of **Just Nuisance,** a Great Dane adopted as a mascot by the Royal Navy during World War II. Just Nuisance apparently liked his pint of beer and would accompany sailors on the train into Cape Town. He had the endearing habit of leading drunken sailors—and only sailors— that he found in the city back to the station in time to catch the last train. The navy went so far as to induct him into the service as an able seaman attached to the HMS *Afrikander*. He died at the age of seven in April 1944 and was given a military funeral. Just below Jubilee Square is the newly built Simonstown Waterfront Centre, with numerous artsy shops, including a Just Nuisance store, where you can buy a present for your pooch back home.

NEED A BREAK? **BERTHAS RESTAURANT** (Wharf's Rd., Simonstown, tel. 021/ 786–2138) serves excellent meals overlooking the jetty, where charter boats take off for whale-watching (in season) and trips to Cape Point. The attached coffee shop has just as good a view and serves light lunches and teas.

PENGUIN POINT CAFE (Boulders Beach parking lot, tel. 021/ 786–1758) has a huge veranda with views over False Bay. It serves hearty breakfasts, light lunches, teas, and dinner. There's a full bar, and it's a great place to watch the sun set—if you're sharp, you'll remember that you're facing east, not west, but don't let that deter you. False Bay sunsets are spectacular. Consisting mostly of reflected light, they are pastel pink, pale blue, lavender, and gold, unlike the more common red and orange variety.

50 TAFELBERG ROAD. The road crosses the northern side of Table Mountain before ending at Devil's Peak. From the Kloof Nek intersection you can descend to Cape Town directly or return to Camps Bay and follow the coastal road back to the city. This route takes you through the beautiful seaside communities of Clifton and Bantry Bay and then along the seaside promenade in Sea Point.

34 TOKAI MANOR. Built in 1795, this is one of the finest Cape Dutch homes in the country. Famed architect Louis Michel Thibault designed its facade. The homestead is reputedly haunted by a horseman who died when he tried to ride his horse down the curving front steps during a drunken revel. You can stop for a look, but the house is not open to the public.

47 WORLD OF BIRDS. Here you can walk through aviaries housing 450 species of indigenous and exotic birds, including eagles, vultures, penguins, and flamingos. No cages separate you from most of the birds, so you can get some pretty good photographs; however, the big raptors are kept behind fences. *Valley Rd., Hout Bay, tel. 021/790–2730, www.worldofbirds.org.za. R28. Daily 9–6.*

OFF THE BEATEN PATH **DISTRICT SIX MUSEUM** – In the Buitenkant Methodist Church, this museum preserves the memory of one of Cape Town's most vibrant multicultural neighborhoods, destroyed in one of the cruelest acts of the apartheid Nationalist government. District Six was proclaimed a white area in 1966, and existing residents were evicted from their homes, which were razed to make way for a white suburb. The people were forced to resettle in bleak outlying areas on the Cape Flats. By the 1970s all the buildings, except churches and mosques, had been demolished. A proposal to redevelop the area has been hugely controversial, and only a small housing component, Zonnebloem, and the campus of the Cape Technicon have been built. Much of the ground is still bare—a grim reminder of the past. There are plans to draw former residents back into the area, but the old swinging District Six is a thing of the past. The museum displays street signs, photographs, life stories of the people who lived there, and a huge floor plan, where former residents can identify the site of their homes. *25A Buitenkant St., tel. 021/461–4735 or 021/465–8009, www.districtsix.co.za. Free. Mon.–Sat. 9–4.*

In This Chapter

By Myrna Robins

Updated by Jennifer Stern

eating out

NOWHERE ELSE IN SOUTH AFRICA is the populace so discerning about food, and nowhere else is there such a wide selection of restaurants. Western culinary history in Cape Town dates back more than 300 years—the city was founded specifically to grow food—and that heritage is reflected in the cuisine. A number of restaurants operate in historic town houses and 18th-century wine estates.

Many restaurants are crowded in high season, so it's best to book in advance whenever possible. With the exception of the fancier restaurants in hotels—where a jacket is required—the dress code in Cape Town is casual (but no shorts). Reservations are always a good idea; we mention them only when they're either essential or not accepted. Book as far ahead as you can, and reconfirm as soon as you arrive (large parties should always call ahead to check the reservations policy).

Unless otherwise noted, the restaurants listed in this guide are open daily for lunch and dinner. The restaurants we list are the cream of the crop in each price category.

CATEGORY	COST*
$$$$	more than R65
$$$	R45–R65
$$	R25–R45
$	less than R25

Rates are for a main course.

CITY BOWL

$$$$ ATLANTIC GRILL ROOM. The flagship restaurant at the luxurious Table Bay Hotel holds a prime position at the city's waterfront development. The room is decorated with updated colonial elegance, and seating on the terrace has views of working docks against a mountain backdrop. Menus combine Asian and European elements with local ingredients like crayfish and venison. First courses include a terrine of baby leeks and langoustines with a pepperoni-almond dressing. For a main course tournedos of eland (venison) are partnered with wild-mushroom duxelles, juniper-berry sauce, and tempura vegetables. For dessert, fruity Asian-inspired creations are artistically displayed. The extensive wine list presents the best of the Cape. *Table Bay Hotel, Quay 6, V&A Waterfront, tel. 021/406–5688. AE, DC, MC, V. Closed Mon.*

$$$$ BLUE DANUBE. Updated Western and central European classics dominate the menu at this former private home on the city perimeter. Talented chef Thomas Sinn's fare is an essential activity on the itineraries of many visitors. Complimentary appetizers precede starters like duck spring rolls on curried lentils. Robust main courses include *crepinettes* (meat wrapped in caul fat) of springbok (venison) with shallot sauce and roast rack of Karoo lamb teamed with a potato gratin. Indulge in Kaiserschmarrn (an Austrian pancake torn into pieces and fried with sugar) with ice cream for dessert. Unhurried, professional service and a carefully selected wine list are hallmarks here. *102 New Church St., Tamboerskloof, tel. 021/423–3624. AE, DC, MC, V. Closed Sun. No lunch Mon. and Sat.*

$$$$ ROZENHOF. Within easy walking distance of the hotels in Gardens, this late 18th-century town house has one of the best wine selections in town. Yellowwood ceilings and brass chandeliers evoke the historic Cape. The restaurant is noted for the consistently good quality of its Asian- and Mediterranean-inspired cuisine and for friendly service. Popular classics include cheese soufflé sauced with mustard cream and a quartet of innovative summer

cape town dining

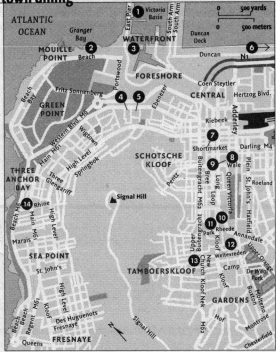

A South African Food Glossary

BILTONG. An integral part of South African life, biltong is air-dried meat cured with vinegar, salt, and spices, and hung to dry. Biltong comes in strips, chunks, or grated and served on bread with butter.

BOBOTIE. A classic Cape Malay dish consisting of delicately spiced ground beef or lamb topped with a savory custard.

BOEREWORS. Afrikaans for farmer's sausage (pronounced "boo-rah-vorse"), this coarse, flavorful sausage has a distinctive spiciness. It's a standard feature at braais.

BREDIE. Bredie is a slow-cooked stew, usually made with lamb and green beans, tomatoes, or waterblommetjies—indigenous water flowers.

GALJOEN If you see galjoen on a menu, order it. It's South Africa's national fish—endemic, not very common, and distinctive in taste and texture, with lightly marbled flesh.

GATSBY. Eaten on the streets of Cape Town (and only in Cape Town), this is a whole loaf of bread cut in half lengthwise and filled with fish or meat with lettuce, tomato, and french fries.

LINE FISH. This is a restaurant term for fish caught on a line, as opposed to a net; the assumption is that quality is better as a result.

PERI-PERI. A condiment and marinade introduced by Portuguese immigrants from Mozambique, peri-peri sauce is made with the searing hot piri-piri chili. There are as many recipes as there are uses.

POTJIE. Sometimes called potjiekos, this is a type of stew (pronounced "poy-key"), simmered in a three-legged wrought-iron cooking pot (the potjie itself).

SOSATIES. In this South African version of a kebab, chunks of meat are marinated in Cape Malay spices and grilled.

salads. Crispy roast duck with a choice of fruity sauces is a time-honored favorite. Layers of local Gorgonzola and mascarpone with preserved figs and a glass of port are a savory-sweet alternative to finales like ginger-and-lemongrass ice cream encased in coconut-and-lime biscuits. *18 Kloof St., tel. 021/424–1968. AE, DC, MC, V. Closed Sun. No lunch Sat.*

$$$–$$$$ CAPE COLONY RESTAURANT. Tall bay windows, a high domed ceiling, and a giant trompe l'oeil mural—an inventive evocation of Table Mountain—befit this historic and unashamedly colonial hotel. Renowned chef Garth Stroebel creates stylish contemporary fare based on southern African ingredients. Most dishes are given voguish treatment, while others reflect indigenous Cape Malay flavors. The best seafood choices are first courses like crayfish bisque served with shrimp *bruschetta*. Smoked crocodile, carpaccio of spiced ostrich, and a guinea-fowl Waldorf salad are starters that star the continent's exotic items. Karoo loin of lamb with Moroccan spices is a popular entrée. The best South African vintages are supplemented by French champagnes. *Orange St., Gardens, tel. 021/483–1000. Reservations essential. AE, DC, MC, V. No lunch.*

$$$–$$$$ PANAMA JACK'S. Nowhere in town will you find bigger crayfish than at this this raw-timber structure in the heart of the docks with loud music, crowded tables, and a nonexistent decor. Choose your entrée from large open tanks, and it is weighed, then grilled or steamed. Expect to pay about R30 per 100 grams (R300 a kilogram) for this delicacy or for the extra-large black tiger prawns. There is plenty of less expensive seafood, including daily specials such as baby squid and local line fish. It can be difficult to find this place at night, so lunch may be a better option. *Royal Yacht Club basin, off Goliath Rd., Docks, tel. 021/447–3992. AE, DC, MC, V. No lunch Sat.*

$$$–$$$$ QUAY WEST. This Cape Grace Hotel restaurant overlooks the bascule bridge gateway to the waterfront yacht basin and has comfortable wicker chairs and crisp table settings. Starters—many of which could double as a light supper—include smoked venison salad, biltong-and-feta soufflé, and a warm crocodile salad. For a main course try free-range roast chicken with grilled polenta and Mediterranean vegetables or grilled Norwegian salmon with a coconut-and-lobster reduction. Desserts include Cape brandy pudding with marmalade ice cream. The wine list is well annotated, and the popular Bascule bar stocks more than 300 varieties of whiskey. The lunch menu varies significantly from dinner; the breakfast buffet is a local favorite. *Cape Grace Hotel, West Quay, V&A Waterfront, tel. 021/418–0520. AE, DC, MC, V.*

$$$–$$$$ TOBAGOS. A series of intimate areas compose this restaurant, and a vast deck makes room for cocktails and alfresco meals. Executive chef Jeffrie Siew, who has launched several top South African hotel restaurants, moves effortlessly from Asian to Western cuisines. Chicken *satay* is dressed with peanut sauce, and the Cape's star ingredient, crayfish, is given Italian treatment and grilled with pesto and a white-wine risotto. The trendy dessert list includes a dark chocolate mousse in an envelope of cacao and teamed with pistachio ice cream. *Radisson Hotel Waterfront, Beach Rd., Granger Bay, tel. 021/418–5729. AE, DC, MC, V.*

$$–$$$$ BUKHARA. Delectable and authentic northern Indian fare is served at this hugely popular restaurant above a pedestrian mall lined with antiques shops and stalls. Red walls and dark furniture do little to minimize the cavernous interior, which has an open kitchen. Delicious garlic nan bread precedes selections from the tandoor oven or a curry. Lamb marinated with yogurt and spices pleases sensitive palates. Prawns come in several guises; the spicy coconut curry with tamarind is a firm favorite. Equally good vegetarian options, such as *tandoori* homemade cheese and vegetables, are inexpensive. *33 Church St., tel. 021/424–0000. Reservations essential. AE, DC, MC, V. No lunch Sun.*

$$$ AFRICA CAFE. Multicolored cloths and hand-glazed crockery complement the vibrant cusine at this restored 18th-century city square restaurant. The communal feast originates from all corners of Africa. There are no entrées, but rather a tasty series of patties, dips, puffs, and pastries accompanied by dips, along with dishes like Moroccan lamb and date stew and Cape Malay chicken *biryani*. Vegetarian dishes are profuse. The Soweto *chakalaka* is a fiery example of a cooked vegetable relish. Meals are prix fixe at R95 a person. Cape wines are available. Try *umqomboti* beer for an authentic accompaniment. The Zulu Room, with its adjoining roof deck, has spectacular sunset views. *108 Shortmarket St., tel. 021/422–0221. AE, DC, MC, V. Closed Sun. No lunch.*

$$–$$$ WANGTHAI. Authentic Thai restaurants like this one continue to flourish though the trend for this cuisine has passed its peak. *Tom yum goong* (spicy prawns in a lemongrass-scented broth) is a top starter, as is an eggplant dish beautifully spiced with chili and basil. Beef, pork, and chicken stir-fries of beef vie with deep-fried fish served with sweet-and-sour, hot, and mild sauces or pungent red and green curries, tempered by coconut milk and mounds of sticky rice. The restaurant has an open kitchen, and it occupies a prime spot on a trendy late-night strip between the city and the Atlantic seaboard. *105 Paramount Pl., Main Rd., Green Point, tel. 021/ 439–6164. AE, DC, MC, V. No lunch Sat.*

$–$$ CAFE MOZART. This continental-style café and coffee shop is a 30-year-old institution. Walls are lined with mirrors and music-themed posters, and tables are dressed with lace cloths. Regulars head inside, while the passing trade sits under umbrellas at pavement tables. Breakfast is served all day, and the menu has a good selection of sandwiches and salads. But it's the daily specials—the soups in particular—that most diners choose. Featherlight quiches, smoked salmon and Brie for one, come with fresh salad. Decadent desserts, made daily, are usually sold out by 2. Mozart's version of lemon meringue gives new meaning to this familiar favorite. *37 Church St., tel./fax 021/424–3774. Reservations essential. AE, DC, MC, V. Closed Sun. No dinner. BYOB.*

$–$$ OCEAN BASKET. On Restaurant Mile along the city fringe, this informal eatery has few competitors in the field of bargain-price, ocean-fresh seafood. You can sit facing the street or in the courtyard at the back. Calamari—stewed, curried, pickled, or in a salad—

is a prominet appetizer. The catch of the day is listed on the many blackboards, but delicately flavored hake-and-chips is the budget draw card. Standard entrées range from Cajun-style grilled calamari to a huge seafood platter for two. Greek salads are authentic. Desserts are average. *75 Kloof St., tel. 021/422–0322. Reservations not accepted. AE, DC, MC, V.*

ATLANTIC COAST

$$$$ THE RESTAURANT. Although neither the name nor the decor would win prizes for originality, the same cannot be said for the brilliant cutting-edge cuisine. You won't find chicken or beef on the menu. Instead, try seared oysters and foie gras on brioche with Cape brandy cream or, for half the price, an equally delectable appetizer of goat cheese baklava. Line fish, sauced with passion fruit and grilled venison served with red cabbage, a celeriac rosti, and wild tea and red-currant sauce, are both excellent. The red China pork and prawns braised with rock candy and shiitake mushrooms get rave reviews. *51a Somerset Rd., Green Point, tel. 021/419–2921. Reservations essential. AE, DC, MC, V. Closed Sun. No lunch.*

$$$–$$$$ SAN MARCO. Restaurants open and close in Cape Town with alarming speed, but this Italian institution in Sea Point has been a meeting place for generations, since it first opened as a gelateria. Come not for the decor but for the consistency and authenticity of dishes conjured by the original chef. Grilled calamari is superb and homemade pasta is topped with simple, flavorful sauces. Luxurious langoustines are well priced. The veal dishes are especially good. If a less common Cape line fish such as elf (shad) is available, don't miss it. Finish with one of the renowned ice creams or sorbets, which are dressed with a splash of liqueur. *92 Main Rd., Sea Point, tel. 021/439–2758. Reservations essential. AE, DC, MC, V. Closed Tues. No lunch Mon.–Sat.*

$$–$$$$ BLUES. Doors open to frame an inviting vista of palms, sand, and azure sea from the balcony of this popular restaurant. The mood and menu are largely Californian, but appetizers such as

cape peninsula dining

Metro

Table Bay

See Cape Town Dining Map

1 — 14

PARDEN EILAND

N1

FORESHORE

ATLANTIC OCEAN

Bantry Bay

M3

OBSERVATORY

Campse Bay

N2

15

Bakoven

NEWLANDS

RONDEBOSCH

16

CLAREMONT

M6 Victoria

BISHOPSCOURT

KENILWORTH

17

Rhodes

WYNBERG

Llandudno

18

PLUMSTEAD

Main

CONSTANTIA

Hout Bay

19

20 **21**

M4

Duiker Island

Hout Bay

Chapmans Peak

22

23

M3

Main

M5

RETREAT

WESTLAKE

LAKESIDE

Muizenberg

M6

Silvermine Nature Reserve

M64

24

Sun Valley

25

N

26

0   2 miles

Kommetjie Main

Fish Hoek

Fish Hoek Basin

0   3 km

smoked springbok (venison) add African flair. The pasta is deservedly popular, and spaghettini with saffron cream, black mussels, and baby fennel is not only delicious, but also the most affordable entrée on the menu. Lamb chops are served with an eggplant, caper, and olive relish and the seafood platter is luxurious but pricey. Popular desserts include the chocolate pecan brownie with vanilla ice cream and hot chocolate sauce. *The Promenade, Victoria Rd., Camps Bay, tel. 021/438–2040. Reservations essential. AE, DC, MC, V.*

SOUTHERN SUBURBS

$$$$ AU JARDIN. Tucked away in a corner of the historic Vineyard hotel in Newlands, complete with fountain and views of Table Mountain, this restaurant serves classic French cuisine with subtle Cape and Mediterranean accents. Appetizers might include smoked kudu (venison) and garlic terrine or mille-feuille of eggplant and tomato with a mushroom sauce. Panfried beef fillet is paired with savoy cabbage and lyonnaise potatoes. Apart from classic finales, desserts include innovative guava-and-coconut sabayon with rum-raisin ice cream. There's a menu dégustation, and the à la carte menu at lunch is a good value. *Vineyard Hotel, Colinton Rd., Claremont, tel. 021/683–1520. AE, DC, MC, V. Closed Sun. No lunch Sat. and Mon.*

$$$$ BUITENVERWACHTING. On a historic wine estate, this superb
★ restaurant is consistently rated among the country's best. Some tables have views of the vineyards sloping toward the mountains. Menus change daily, but imaginative starters might include a timbale of wild and cultivated mushrooms with rabbit and a balsamic, honey, and thyme jus. Guinea fowl with a creamy leek-and-shiitake tagliatelle is teamed with a beetroot-and-apple salad and loin of springbok (venison) is crowned with a truffle-and-mushroom sauce. Local fruits star in imaginative desserts, as in the grapefruit granita with pawpaw-and-guava salad. Vegetarians can relish a five-course dinner menu or a three-course lunch menu. *Klein Constantia Rd., Constantia, tel. 021/794–*

3522. *Reservations essential. AE, DC, MC, V. Closed Sun.–Mon. and July. No lunch Sat.*

$$$$ THE CELLARS. Highly professional service complements artful presentation at this restaurant in the historic Cellars-Hohenort Hotel. Menu items are understated in their descriptions, belying the quality of the food created by renowned British chef Phil Alcook, which maximizes fresh, seasonal ingredients. Green peas team with foie gras in an unusual soup and poached salmon with cauliflower is sauced with horseradish cream. For a main course try the slow-roasted cannon of lamb with a herb puree and ratatouille or the char-grilled fillet of ostrich with bubble and squeak (cabbage and potatoes). For dessert there's tart Tatin with five-spice ice cream. The wine list is extensive. *15 Hohenort Ave., Constantia, tel. 021/794–2137. Reservations essential. AE, DC, MC, V.*

$$$$ CONSTANTIA UITSIG. This restaurant in a restored farmstead attracts a large, loyal following. Reserve a table on the enclosed veranda for tremendous mountain views. The menu is a blend of northern Italian and Provençal cuisines. Carpaccio comes in both fish and beef versions. Many diners start with homemade pasta before going on to main courses like line fish served with crisp cabbage and a spicy sauce or sweetbreads sautéed with bacon, peas, mushrooms and Marsala. Desserts include iced berries with a hot white chocolate sauce. *Spaanschemat River Rd., Constantia, tel. 021/794–4480. Reservations essential. AE, DC, MC, V. No lunch Mon.*

$$$$ PARKS. Jam-packed since it opened, this restored Victorian villa is convivial and elegant. Michael Olivier's zesty contemporary cuisine strikes the right chord. Local Camembert is baked with tomato and eggplant in phyllo, and Cape salmon trout gravlax is seared and teamed with new potatoes and a beetroot salsa. Blackened Cajun-style fish is served with herbed crème fraîche and ostrich fillet Wellington is accompanied by bush-tea-flavored polenta and juniper-berry sauce. Desserts are obligatory: crème brûlée is garnished with poached dried apricots and panna cotta is served with caramelized blood orange. There's a good choice of wines by the glass. *114 Constantia Rd., Constantia, tel. 021/797–8202. Reservations essential. AE, DC, MC, V. Closed Sun. No lunch Sat.*

$$$–$$$$ **★** **LA COLOMBE.** This Provençal restaurant is collecting accolades for its southern French fare. French doors in the sunshine-yellow and sky-blue dining room open onto a courtyard. The native French chef transforms local produce into flavorful renderings of *pan bagna* (salad niçoise on French bread) or carpaccio of tuna with a sweet tomato sauce. Entrées include a satisfying peasant dish of grilled sausage and soybeans with a baby marrow puree or upmarket grilled noisettes of springbok (venison) in honey jus with Cape Malay spice. The wicked terrine of dark chocolate is further enriched with caramel sauce. *Uitsig Farm, Spaanschemat River Rd., Constantia, tel. 021/794–2390. Reservations essential. AE, DC, MC, V. Closed Tues. No dinner Sun.*

$$$–$$$$ **STEENBERG.** The original winery stands on this historic estate, which also serves the 18th-century manor house hotel across the court. Cozy tables are set in alcoves created from the original vats. Executive chef Garth Almazan does not compromise on quality. First courses include seafood *laksa* (rice noodles with spicy coconut milk sauce) and warm Asian ostrich salad with glass noodles and Japanese ginger. Winter specials of oxtail casserole and slow-braised lamb shank are always in demand. A spiked crème brûlée is one of the most popular finales. There's an excellent selection of estate wines by the glass. *Steenberg Hotel, Steenberg Rd., Tokai, tel. 021/713–2222. AE, DC, MC, V.*

$$$ **JONKERSHUIS.** Classic Cape hospitality is put forth in this 19th-century building adjoining the manor house at the Cape's oldest wine estate. Fresh line fish and roast loin of lamb share the menu with classic *bobotie* (spiced minced beef with dried fruit and nut slivers topped with a savory baked custard) and *smoorsnoek* (a popular Cape fish) braised with onion, potato, and chili. The chicken pie is made from a recipe handed down through generations of Dutch settlers. To taste all these dishes, ask for a Cape sampler. Jonkershuis also serves hearty breakfasts and light

Eating Well Is the Best Revenge

Eating out is a major part of every travel experience. It's a chance to explore flavors you don't find at home. And often the walking you do on vacation means that you can dig in without guilt.

START AT THE TOP By all means take in a really good restaurant or two while you're on the road. A trip is a time to kick back and savor the pleasures of the palate. Read up on the culinary scene before you leave home. Check out representative menus on the Web—some chefs have gone electronic. And ask friends who have just come back. Then reserve a table as far in advance as you can, remembering that the best establishments book up months in advance. Remember that some good restaurants require you to reconfirm the day before or the day of your meal. Then again, some really good places will call you, so make sure to leave a number where you can be reached.

ADVENTURES IN EATING A trip is the perfect opportunity to try food you can't get at home. So leave yourself open to try an ethnic food that's not represented where you live or to eat fruits and vegetables you've never heard of. One of them may become your next favorite food.

BEYOND GUIDEBOOKS You can rely on the restaurants you find in these pages. But also look for restaurants on your own. When you're ready for lunch, ask people you meet where they eat. Look for tiny holes-in-the-wall with a loyal following and the best burgers or crispiest pizza crust. Find out about local chains whose fame rests upon a single memorable dish. There's hardly a food-lover who doesn't relish the chance to share a favorite place. It's fun to come up with your own special find—and asking about food is a great way to start a conversation.

SAMPLE LOCAL FLAVORS Do check out the specialties. Is there a special brand of ice cream or a special dish that you simply must try?

HAVE A PICNIC Every so often eat al fresco. Grocery shopping gives you a whole different view of a place.

refreshments. *Groot Constantia Estate, Main Rd., Constantia, tel. 021/ 794–6255. Reservations essential. AE, DC, MC. No dinner Sun.–Mon.*

FALSE BAY

$$–$$$$ **BERTHA'S RESTAURANT AND COFFEEHOUSE.** View sparkling water against a mountain backdrop as you dine alfresco and watch boating activities from the naval dockyard and yacht club. Good use is made of local produce in the contemporary dishes, like Atlantic black mussels poached in chili-sparked, thyme-scented white wine. Pizzas, steak, and ribs are popular, but seafood, pasta, and chicken satays make tempting alternatives. In demand is the inexpensive fried hake in beer batter with chips (french fries). The double chocolate tart with mascarpone cream cheese gets rave reviews. Lunch is popular, so it's a good idea to reserve in advance. *1 Wharf Rd., Simonstown, tel. 021/786–2138. AE, DC, MC, V.*

$$ **BRASS BELL.** Whether you eat in the main restaurant, in the cabin, on the terrace, or in the gazebo, you have views of False Bay, frolicking surfers, and fishing boats heading for the harbor. This informal place can get crowded and noisy. There's a choice of four menus: the main restaurant presents formal fare, the other areas keep to lighter, more casual meals. All have a good value for the money. The emphasis is on fish and seafood, but the menu appeases vegetarians and carnivores as well. The fare is straightforward, enlivened by a few traditional Cape and Mediterranean dishes. *Waterfront, Kalk Bay, tel. 021/788–5456. AE, DC, MC, V.*

$$ **OLYMPIA CAFE.** Long a well-kept secret among regulars, this tiny eatery is between antiques shops opposite the fishing harbor. Plan on a wait to be seated at one of the 10 mismatched tables. The quality of the mostly Mediterranean fare is consistently high and the prices astonishingly low. A seasonal favorite are the eggplant rolls, filled either with butternut squash and ricotta, or sweet potato and ricotta, both with piquant tomato sauce. Rare tuna steak with mashed potatoes and ratatouille is delectable. The chef serves more than 12,000 omelets each year, accompanied by excellent croissants and crusty loaves from the cafe's bakery up the road. *134 Main Rd., Kalk Bay, tel. 021/788–6396. Reservations not accepted. No credit cards. Closed Mon. No dinner Tues.–Wed. and Sun.*

In This Chapter

Updated by Jennifer Stern

shopping

TRADITIONAL ARTS AND CRAFTS can be very good buys in Cape Town. Many items sold here come from Zululand or neighboring countries. Street vendors, particularly on St. George's Mall and Greenmarket Square, often sell the same curios for half the price. If you look around, you can also find some excellent clothing buys, ranging from traditional "African chic" outfits to haute couture and including, of course, some very well made and reasonably priced outdoor goods.

Be wary of cheap imitations: "ebony" carvings often achieve their black luster through the use of shoe polish. Real ebony is heavy, and you can't scratch the black off—although think hard before buying it, anyway, as wood carving is contributing to the deforestation of Africa. Ivory is freely sold in South Africa to local residents, but don't be tempted to buy any, as you won't be able to get it through customs. Note too, that if you buy carvings from hippo teeth, you may need to do some smart talking to get them across borders—to the untrained eye they are almost indistinguishable from ivory.

MARKETS
GREENMARKET SQUARE. You can get good buys on clothing, T-shirts, handcrafted silver jewelry, and locally made leather shoes and sandals. It's lively and fun whether or not you buy anything. *Mon.–Sat. 9–4:30.*

WATERFRONT TRADING COMPANY. In this indoor market more than 140 artists show their work, an assortment of handcrafted jewelry, rugs, glass, pottery, and leather shoes and sandals. *Waterfront, tel. 021/408–7842. Daily 9:30–6.*

SPECIALTY STORES

African Art

AFRICAN IMAGE. Look here for colorful cloth from Nigeria and Ghana, West African masks, Malian blankets, and beaded designs from southern African tribes. A variety of Zulu baskets are also available at moderate prices. *Burg and Church Sts., tel./fax 021/423–8385. Weekdays 8:45–5, Sat. 9–1:30.*

THE PAN-AFRICAN MARKET. The market extends over two floors of a huge building and is a jumble of tiny stalls, traditional African hairdressers and tailors, potters, artists, musicians, and drummers. There is also a small, very African restaurant. *76 Long St., tel. 021/426–4478. Weekdays 9–5, Sat. 9–3.*

African Clothing and Fabrics

MNANDI TEXTILES. Here you'll find a range of African fabrics, including traditional West African prints and Dutch wax prints. The store sells ready-made and made-to-order African clothing for adults and children. *90 Station Rd., tel. 021/447–6814, fax 021/447–7937. Weekdays 9–5, Sat. 9–1.*

N.C.M. FASHIONS–AFRICAN PRIDE. This is the place to go for traditional clothing from all over Africa. One of the most striking outfits is the brightly colored *bubu,* a loose-fitting garment with a matching head wrap. You can buy off the rack or order a custom outfit. *173 Main Rd., Claremont, tel. 021/683–1022. Weekdays 9–5:30, Sat. 9–1:30.*

Books

CLARKE'S BOOKSHOP. A local favorite, Clarke's has a fantastic collection of Africana books, a good selection of antiquarian titles, and some esoterica. 211 Long St., tel. 021/423–5739. *Weekdays 9–5, Sat. 9–1.*

EXCLUSIVE BOOKS. This is one of the best all-around bookshops in the country. The chain carries a wide selection of coffee-table books on Africa and periodicals. Browse at the coffee bar if you like. Be prepared to pay at least twice as much for books here as you would in the United States or Britain. *Shop 225, Victoria Wharf, Waterfront, tel. 021/419–0905. Mon.–Thurs. 9 AM–10:30 PM, Fri.–Sat. 9 AM–11 PM, Sun. 10–9. Lower Mall, Cavendish Sq., Claremont, tel. 021/674–3030. Mon.–Thurs. 9–9, Fri.–Sat. 9 AM–11 PM, Sun. 10–9.*

Wine

Many wineries will mail your wine purchases to your home, as will the major wine shops. You are allowed a maximum of 24 bottles per person, at a cost of US$10 a bottle. Shipping takes about two weeks. Many high-quality wines are under $20 at local shops.

STEVEN ROM. Have purchases shipped to your home or buy directly from the Web site. (*Checkers Galleria Centre, 76 Regent Rd., Sea Point, South Africa, tel. 021/439–6043, www.wineseller.co.za*).

VAUGHAN JOHNSON'S WINE SHOP. Former grape grower Vaughn Johnson hand-selects Cape wines for his high-profile shop. Overseas delivery is available. (*Pier Head, Dock Rd., Waterfront, tel. 021/419–2121, www.vaughanjohnson.com*).

In This Chapter

Updated by Jennifer Stern

outdoor activities and sports

IN THIS, **THE ADVENTURE CAPITAL OF THE UNIVERSE,** you can dive, paddle, fly, jump, run, slide, fin, walk, or clamber. **ADVENTURE VILLAGE** (tel. 021/424–1580, www.adventure-village.co.za) books a range of activities from its offices at the top of Long Street, which it shares with Abseil Africa. **AFRICAN ADVENTURE TRAVEL CENTRE** (tel. 021/424–1037, www.abisa.co.za) is a multiactivity center in Long Street that offers general travel advice, a bureau de change, Internet café, and adventure booking.

BEACHES

With panoramic views of mountains tumbling to the ocean, the sandy beaches of the Cape Peninsula are stunning and are a major draw for Capetonians and visitors alike. Beautiful as the beaches may be, don't expect to spend hours splashing in the surf. The water around Cape Town is very, very cold, but you get used to it. Beaches on the Atlantic are washed by the Benguela Current flowing up from the Antarctic, and in midsummer the water hovers around 10°C–15°C (50°F–60°F). The water on the False Bay side is usually 5°C (9°F) warmer. Cape beaches are renowned for their clean, snow-white powdery sand. Beachcombers will find every kind of beach to suit them, from intimate coves to sheltered bays and wild, wide beaches stretching forever. If you are looking for more tropical water temperatures, head for the warm Indian Ocean waters of KwaZulu–Natal or the Garden Route.

The major factor that affects any day at a Cape beach is wind. In summer howling southeasters, known as the Cape Doctor, are all too common and can ruin a trip to the beach; during these gales you're better off at Clifton or Llandudno, on the Atlantic side, or the sheltered but very small St. James Beach, on the False Bay side, and maybe even the southern corner of Fish Hoek Beach or one of the pools along Jagers Walk. Boulders and Seaforth are also often sheltered from the southeaster.

Every False Bay community has its own beach, but most are not reviewed here. In comparison with Atlantic beaches, most of them are rather small and often crowded, sandwiched between the sea and the commuter rail line, with Fish Hoek a major exception. South of Simonstown, the beaches tend to be more wild and less developed, except for the very popular Seaforth and Millers Point beaches. At many beaches there may be powerful waves, strong undertow, and dangerous riptides. Lifeguards work the main beaches, but only on weekends and during school breaks. Other beaches are unpatrolled. Although it is nice to stroll along a lonely beach, remember it's risky to wander off on your own in a deserted area.

Atlantic Coast

The beaches below are listed from north to south and are marked on the Cape Peninsula map in the Here and There chapter.

BLOUBERG. Make the 25-km (16-mi) trip north from the city to the other side of Table Bay, and you'll be rewarded with an exceptional (and the most famous) view of Cape Town and Table Mountain. It's divided into two parts: Big Bay, which hosts surfing and sailboarding contests; and Little Bay, better suited to sunbathers and families. It's frequently windy here, which is fine if you want to fly a kite but a nuisance otherwise. (Buy a brightly colored high-tech number at the Kite Shop in Victoria Wharf at the waterfront and relive your childhood.) Swim in front of the lifeguard club. The lawns of the Blue Peter Hotel are a favorite sunset cocktail spot, especially with tired windsurfers. *Follow N1 north toward Paarl and then R27 to Milnerton and Bloubergstrand.*

CLIFTON. This is where the "in" crowd comes to see and be seen. Some of the Cape's most desirable houses cling to the slopes above the beach, and elegant yachts often anchor in the calm water beyond the breakers. Granite outcroppings divide the beach into four segments, imaginatively known as First, Second, Third, and Fourth beaches. Fourth Beach is popular with families, while the others support a strong social and singles scene. Swimming is reasonably safe here, although the undertow is strong and the water, again, freezing. Lifeguards are on duty. On weekends and in peak season Clifton can be a madhouse, and your chances of finding parking at these times are nil. If you plan to visit the beaches in midsummer, consider renting a scooter or motorcycle instead of a car or taking a shuttle from your hotel. *Off Victoria Rd., Clifton. Hout Bay bus from OK Bazaars on Adderley St.*

CAMPS BAY. The spectacular western edge of Table Mountain, known as the Twelve Apostles, provides the backdrop for this long, sandy beach that slopes gently to the water from a grassy verge. The surf is powerful, and there are no lifeguards, but sunbathers can cool off in a tidal pool or under cool outdoor showers. The popular bars and restaurants of Camps Bay lie only yards away across Victoria Road. One drawback is the wind, which can blow hard here. *Victoria Rd. Hout Bay bus from OK Bazaars on Adderley St.*

LLANDUDNO. Die-hard fans return to this beach again and again, and who can blame them? Its setting, among giant boulders at the base of a mountain, is glorious, and sunsets here attract their own aficionados. The surf can be very powerful on the northern side of the beach (where you'll find all the surfers, of course), but the southern side is fine for a quick dip—and in this water that's all you'll want. Lifeguards are on duty on weekends and in season. If you come by bus, brace yourself for a long walk down (and back up) the mountain from the bus stop on the M6. Parking is a nightmare, but most hotels run shuttles during summer. *Llandudno exit off M6 and follow signs. Hout Bay bus from OK Bazaars on Adderley St.*

SANDY BAY. Backed by wild dunes, Cape Town's unofficial nudist beach is also one of its prettiest. Sunbathers can hide among rocky coves or frolic on a long stretch of sandy beach. Shy nudists will appreciate its isolation, 20 minutes on foot from the nearest parking area in Llandudno. Wind, however, can be a problem: if you're caught in the buff when the southeaster starts to blow, you're in for a painful sandblasting. Getting here by bus means a very long walk going down and up the mountain; parking is very difficult. *Llandudno exit off M6 and follow signs to Sandy Bay. Hout Bay bus from OK Bazaars on Adderley St.*

HOUT BAY. This beach appears to have it all: a knockout view of the mountains, gentle surf, and easy access to the restaurants and bars of Mariner's Wharf. The reality is not quite so stunning, with the town's industrial fishing harbor and its mini-oil slicks and other waste products nearby. *Off the M6, Hout Bay. Hout Bay bus from OK Bazaars on Adderley St.*

LONG BEACH. This may be the most impressive beach on the peninsula, a vast expanse of white sand stretching 6½ km (4 mi) from the base of Chapman's Peak to Kommetjie. It's also one of the wildest and least populated, backed by a lagoon and private nature reserve. Because of the wind, it attracts horseback riders and walkers rather than sunbathers, and the surfing is excellent. There is no bus service. *Off M6, Noordhoek.*

False Bay

MUIZENBERG. Once the fashionable resort of South African high society, this long, sandy beach has lost much of its glamour and now appeals to families and beginner surfers. A tacky pavilion houses a swimming pool, water slides, toilets, changing rooms, and snack shops. The beach is lined with colorful bathing boxes of the type once popular at British resorts. Lifeguards are on duty, and the sea is shallow and reasonably safe. *Off the M4.*

FISH HOEK. With the southern corner protected from the southeaster by Elsies Peak, this sandy beach attracts retirees, who appreciate the calm, clear water—it may be the safest bathing beach in the Cape. The middle and northern end of the beach is popular with catamaran sailors and sailboarders, who often stage regattas offshore. Jager Walk, a pathway that runs along the rocky coastline, begins at the beach's southern end.

PARTICIPANT SPORTS

Abseiling (Rappelling)

ABSEIL AFRICA (tel. 021/424–1580, www.adventure-village. co.za) offers a 350-ft abseil off the top of Table Mountain for about R200, not including cable car, and over a waterfall in the mountains about an hour's drive away for about R400–R450, including transportation and lunch.

Aerobatic Flight

To fly upside down in an aerobatic plane, contact **AIR COMBAT CAPE TOWN** (tel. 083/462–0570). Costs range from about R800 to R1,000.

Climbing

Cape Town has hundreds of bolted sport routes around the city and peninsula. Both Table Mountain Sandstone and Cape Granite are excellent hard rocks. There are route guides to all the major climbs and a number of climbing schools in Cape Town. **CAPE TOWN SCHOOL OF MOUNTAINEERING** (tel. 021/

671–9604) operate from Orca Industries, a diving and climbing shop in Claremont. The **LEADING EDGE** (tel. 021/715–3999 or 083/309–1554) offers climbing and hiking training and escorted trips in both disciplines. **HIGH ADVENTURE** (tel. 021/447–8036) specializes in climbing in the Cape Town area.

Diving

The diving around the Cape is excellent, with kelp forests, cold-water corals, very brightly colored reef life, and numerous wrecks. An unusual experience is a dive in the Two Oceans Aquarium. CMAS, NAUI, and PADI dive courses are offered by local operators, beginning at about R1,500. **IAIN'S SCUBA SCHOOL** (tel. 021/439–9322 or 082/894–6054) is a good choice for a dive course. **UNDERWATER WORLD** (tel. 021/461–8290) is a dive shop in the city that also offers courses. **ORCA INDUSTRIES** (tel. 021/671–9673) is based in Claremont and offers dive courses and charters. **FARSIDE ADVENTURES** (tel. 021/786–2599), in Simonstown, is conveniently based for False Bay Diving.

Fly-Fishing

You will find no captive-bred, corn-fed trout lurking in sluggish dams near Cape Town. But in the mountains, just an hour or so away, you'll encounter wild and wily fish in wild and wonderful rivers. The season runs from September 1 to May 31. **ULTIMATE ANGLING** (tel. 083/626–0467 or 021/686–6877) offers escorted tours, all the equipment you'll need, and advice.

Golf

Most golf clubs in the Cape accept visitors, but prior booking is essential. Expect to pay R250–R350 for 18 holes and between R120 and R250 per game to rent golf clubs. Most clubs offer equipment rental. The Winelands in particular have some spectacular courses. **CLOVELLY COUNTRY CLUB** (Clovelly Rd., Clovelly, tel. 021/782–6410), near Fish Hoek, is a tight course that requires masterful shot placement from tee to green. **MILNERTON GOLF CLUB** (Bridge Rd., Milnerton, tel. 021/552–1047), sandwiched between the sea and a lagoon, is the Western Cape's only links course and can be difficult when the wind blows. **MOWBRAY GOLF CLUB** (Raapenberg Rd., Mowbray, tel. 021/685–3018), with its great views of Devil's Peak, is a magnificent parkland course that has hosted several major tournaments; there are a number of interesting water holes. Unfortunately, noise from the highway can spoil the atmosphere.

Founded in 1885, **ROYAL CAPE GOLF CLUB** (Ottery Rd., Wynberg, tel. 021/761–6551) is the oldest course in Africa and has hosted the South African Open many times. Its beautiful setting and immaculate fairways and greens make a round here a must for visitors. The club does not rent equipment. The challenging and scenic **STEENBERG GOLF ESTATE** (Steenberg and Tokai Rds., Tokai, tel. 021/713–1632) is the most exclusive and expensive course on the peninsula. A game costs more than R400 per person unless you're staying in the hotel. Dress codes are strictly enforced here.

Hiking and Kloofing (Canyoning)

Cape Town and the surrounding areas offer some of the finest hiking in the world, mostly through the spectacularly beautiful mountains. Kloofing, known as canyoning in the United States, is the practice of following a mountain stream through its gorge, canyon, or kloof by swimming, rock hopping, and jumping over waterfalls or cliffs into deep pools. There are some exceptional kloofing venues in the Cape. **ABSEIL AFRICA** (tel. 021/424–1580, www.adventure-village.co.za) runs a kloofing and abseiling trip on the Steenbras River, better known as Kamakaze Kanyon. **CAPE ECO TRAILS** (tel. 021/785–5511, www.capetrails.com) has various escorted hikes. There is a fantastic overnight hiking trail in the Cape Point section of **CAPE PENINSULA NATIONAL PARK** (tel. 011/780–9526), but you need to book ahead. You can do a sort of pseudo-overnight hike on Table Mountain. **SILVERMIST MOUNTAIN LODGE** (tel. 021/794–7601, www.silvermistmountainlodge.com) can arrange to shuttle you between the Lower Cable Station and the lodge in Constantia—about four–six hours' walk from the Upper Cable Station. You could then spend a comfortable night in one of the cottages with full kitchens at the lodge and walk farther the next day if you like.

Horseback Riding

SLEEPY HOLLOW HORSE RIDING (tel./fax 021/789–2341) offers 1½- and two-hour rides down Long Beach, a 6-km (4-mi) expanse of sand that stretches from Noordhoek Beach to Kommetjie.

Sea Kayaking

COASTAL KAYAK TRAILS (tel. 021/439–1134, www.kayak.co.za) has regular sunset and sunrise paddles off Sea Point. **SEA KAYAKING UNLIMITED** (tel. 021/424–8114, www.faceadrenalin.com) offers regular scenic paddles off Hout Bay to Seal Island and below Chapman's Peak.

Skydiving

You can do a tandem sky dive (no experience necessary) and have your photograph taken hurtling earthward with Table Mountain in the background with **CAPE PARACHUTE CLUB** (tel. 082/800–6290).

SPECTATOR SPORTS

It's easy to get tickets for ordinary club matches and for interprovincial games. Getting tickets to an international test match is more of a challenge; however, there's always somebody selling tickets—at a price, of course.

Cricket and Rugby

The huge sporting complex off Boundary Road in Newlands is the home of the **WESTERN PROVINCE CRICKET UNION** (tel. 021/683–6420). The **WESTERN PROVINCE RUGBY FOOTBALL UNION** (Newlands, tel. 021/689–4921) also has its headquarters at Newlands. Next door to the Newlands sporting complex, in the South African Sports Science Institute, is the **SA RUGBY MUSEUM** (tel. 021/685–3038), open weekdays 9–4.

Sailing

In January 2003, the Cape to Rio Yacht Race takes off. The fun fleet leaves on January 4, and the serious sailors set out a week later, on January 11. Even if you don't follow the whole race, the start is a fantastic spectacle, either from a boat, Robben Island, or the top of Table Mountain.

Soccer

Soccer in South Africa is much more grassroots than cricket or rugby and is very big in the townships. Amateur games are played from March to September at many venues all over the peninsula. Professional games are played from October to April at Greenpoint Stadium, Athlone Stadium, and Newlands. Watch the press for details.

In This Chapter

Updated by Jennifer Stern

nightlife and the arts

YOU CAN ALWAYS FIND SOMETHING TO DO at the waterfront, given that there's more than a dozen cinema screens, 40 restaurants, and 10 bars from which to choose. The rest of the city center, except for isolated restaurants and bars, empties out after business hours, and lone couples may not feel safe walking the deserted streets at night. The big exception is the few square blocks around the intersection of Long and Orange streets, which have become a cauldron of youth-oriented nightclubs, bars, and restaurants. Even here, though, exercise caution late at night. Sea Point, once a major after-dark scene, has lost much of its business to the waterfront. Still, it's here that you can experience contemporary black South African culture and partake in some good music and nightlife.

Schedules and Tickets

The best monthly roundups of entertainment in Cape Town are *Cape Review* and *SA City Life*, which also lists events in Durban and Johannesburg. For weekly updates try "Friday," the entertainment supplement of the *Mail & Guardian*, or the "Top of the Times" in Friday's *Cape Times*. Both are informed, opinionated, and up-to-date. The *Argus* newspaper's "Tonight" section gives you a complete daily listing of what's on, plus contact numbers.

Tickets for almost every cultural and sporting event in the country (including movies) can be purchased through **COMPUTICKET** (tel. 083/909–0909). Cape Town is a very gay-friendly city. For information on the gay scene, contact **AFRICA OUTING** (tel. 021/671–4028 or 083/273–8422, www.afouting.com).

THE ARTS

The **ARTSCAPE** (D. F. Malan St., Foreshore, tel. 021/421–7839 for inquiries; 021/421–7695 for bookings; 083/909–0909 for Computicket, www.artscape.co.za), a huge and unattractive theater complex, is the hub for performing arts and other cultural activities. Cape Town City Ballet and the Cape Town Philharmonic Orchestra, as well as the city's theater and opera companies, make their homes in the center's three theaters. Since 1994 there's been a conscious effort throughout the country to make the performing arts more representative and multicultural. The formerly Eurocentric emphasis has subsided, and today there's a palpable African-arts excitement in the air. Classics are still well represented, as are the latest contemporary worldwide trends. During summer, when the weather's good, Cape Town has its own version of New York City's Central Park's Shakespeare in the Park at the excellent **MAYNARDVILLE OPEN-AIR THEATRE**, in Wynberg. Booking is through Computicket (tel. 083/909–0909). Theatergoers often bring a picnic supper to enjoy before the show.

Classical Music

The **CAPE TOWN PHILHARMONIC ORCHESTRA**, alternates performing at city hall and at the Artscape Theatre Center. The **SPIER SUMMER FESTIVAL** held at the Spier Winery and Hotel in the Winelands takes place between November and February, has a varied program, and performances are held under the stars in an amphitheater at the Spier Wine Estate. You can take Spier's own vintage steam train out to the estate, wine and dine at one of the three restaurants or have a picnic dinner prepared by the estate, then enjoy the show, and return to Cape Town on the train. And in October the attractive village of Franschhoek in the Winelands hosts the Fête de la Musique, featuring many visiting artists, most of them from France. As part of its program to introduce classical music to the general public, the Philharmonic Orchestra also stages a series of lunchtime concerts in the foyer of the Nico complex. Far more exciting, though, would be to watch the orchestra at one of its two appearances at the Kirstenbosch Gardens open-air concerts. They usually do the first and last concerts of the season. The orchestra has hosted several guest conductors from Europe and the United States and has an active program, which includes a summer program of free concerts at the outdoor AGFA Amphitheatre, at the waterfront.

Film

Ster-Kinekor and Nu Metro screen mainstream movies at cinema complexes all over the city. The waterfront alone has two movie houses with 16 screens altogether, which gives you a huge choice. Check newspaper listings for what's playing. At Cavendish Square and the waterfront, the Cinema Nouveau concentrates on showing foreign and art films.

IMAX CINEMA (BMW Pavilion, Waterfront, tel. 021/419–7365, www.imax.co.za), with a giant, nearly hemispherical, five-story screen and six-channel wraparound sound, makes viewers feel as if they're participating in the filmed event. Movies usually concentrate more on visuals than story line, such as wildlife, extreme sports, underwater marine life, or even rock concerts.

The **LABIA** (68 Orange St., Gardens, tel. 021/424–5927, www. labia.co.za) is an independent art house that screens quality mainstream and alternative films, including the works of some of the best European filmmakers. There are four screens. A small coffee bar serves snacks.

Theater

The **BAXTER THEATRE COMPLEX** (Main Rd., Rondebosch, tel. 021/685–7880, www.baxter.co.za) is part of the University of Cape Town and has a reputation for producing serious drama and wacky comedies, as well as some rather experimental stuff.

The complex features a 657-seat theater, a concert hall, a smaller studio, and a restaurant and bar.

NIGHTLIFE

Bars and Pubs

The **PERSEVERANCE TAVERN** (83 Buitenkant St., Gardens, tel. 021/461–2440), which dates to 1836, claims to be the oldest tavern in the city. The facade has been beautifully restored, but you may feel claustrophobic in the small, interconnected rooms; the clientele here is pretty rowdy. The popular **OBZ CAFE** (115 Lower Main Rd., Observatory, tel. 021/448–5555) is a big and funky bar and café with excellent coffee, good food, and cocktails. **LONG STREET CAFE** (259 Long St., tel. 021/424–2464) is a favorite with locals, serving up light tasty dishes, coffee, and, of course, cocktails.

The **SPORTS CAFÉ** (Victoria Wharf, Waterfront, tel. 021/419–5558) is a huge place with large-screen TVs. The bar gets into the spirit of major foreign sporting events like the Super Bowl and the FA Cup Final (England's soccer championship) and is undoubtedly the best place to watch sports in the city. **QUAY FOUR** (Quay 4, tel. 021/419–2008), also at the waterfront, is big with the after-work suit-and-tie brigade, which clogs picnic tables on the wooden deck overlooking the harbor. **FERRYMAN'S** (Dock Rd., V&A Waterfront, tel. 021/419–7748) has a roaring fire inside on winter nights in addition to an outdoor deck area and a suit-and-tie crowd. The restrained but fairly funky crowd leans toward **CAFE ERTE** (265 Main Rd., Three Anchor Bay, tel. 021/434–6624), which is very gay-friendly.

Clubs

Nightclubs in Cape Town change faster than the weather. The area bounded by Loop, Long, Wale, and Orange streets is the best place to get a feeling for what's going on in town. An old diehard is **CORNER HOUSE** (Glynn and Canterbury Sts., no phone), which plays music from the 1980s onward.

For clubs with live music your best bet is **MAMA AFRICA** (Long St., tel. 021/424–8634), with live music Monday through Saturday and usually a marimba band on Wednesday night and authentic African food, authentic African music, and authentic African pulse. Probably the best spot in town is the **DRUM CAFE** (Glynn St., tel. 021/461–1305), which has live performances by percussionists from all over Africa. On Wednesday there is a drum circle and on Monday a women's drum circle (men are welcome but may not drum).

Jazz

Many of the mainstream jazz clubs in the city double as restaurants. Cover charges range from R15 to R30. The **GREEN DOLPHIN JAZZ RESTAURANT** (Waterfront, tel. 021/421–7471) attracts some of the best mainstream musicians in the country as well as a few from overseas. The cover charge is R15–R20. **WINCHESTER MANSIONS HOTEL** (Beach Rd., Sea Point, tel. 021/434–2351) does a mellow Sunday brunch in the courtyard for about R110 with some of the city's best jazz musicians livening the scene. Other than the above, the hot venues change so quickly, it's best to get info when you're here. Cape Town Tourism has a list of good jazz venues and attempts to keep up with the frequent changes.

In This Chapter

Updated by Jennifer Stern

where to stay

FINDING LODGING IN CAPE TOWN CAN BE A NIGHTMARE during high
season (December to January). Travel between April and August,
if you can, to take advantage of off-season discounts. If you arrive
in Cape Town without a reservation, head for Cape Town Tourism's
Information Centre, which has a helpful accommodations desk.

City center hotels are a good option if you're here on business.
By day the historic city center is a vibrant place, but at night, it's
shut up tight. Night owls may prefer the nonstop action of the
redeveloped waterfront. For beauty and tranquility, head to the
southern suburbs, especially Constantia. You'll need a car, and
should plan on 15–30 minutes to get into town. Atlantic Coast
hotels provide the closest thing to a beach vacation, despite the
cold ocean waters.

Keep in mind that international flights from the U.S. and Europe
arrive in the morning and return flights depart in the evening.
Most hotels have an 11 AM checkout, so you may have to wait for
a room if you've just arrived and you may have to vacate your
room hours before your flight. Most hotels try to accommodate
you when business is slow. Some larger hotels have lounges
where you can spend the hours awaiting your flight.

Cape Town is regarded as one of the top backpackers'
destinations in the world, with more than 50 hostels. Contact
BACKPACKER TOURISM, SOUTH AFRICA (BTSA; tel. 021/462–
5888) for information.

The most reliable source of good B&B establishments is the **BED & BREAKFAST BUREAU** (tel. 021/794–0030, fax 021/794–0031, www.bookabed.co.za). The **PORTFOLIO OF PLACES** (tel. 011/880–3414, fax 011/788–4802, www.portfoliocollection.com) publishes a respected list of South Africa's best bed-and-breakfasts.

If you're staying for two or more weeks, consider renting a fully furnished apartment. **HOLIDAY BOOKING SERVICES** (Box 27269, Rhine Rd., 8050, tel. 021/434–8222, www.capeholiday.com) has more than 500 high-quality, furnished, fully stocked apartments on its books.

In the past there was a star grading system for hotels in South Africa. This system was done away with and replaced with a more subjective silver, bronze, and gold system that no one really understood. Then a crystal system was instigated. Remnants of all these systems remain, but none is officially in use. A new grading system was being formulated at this writing.

Assume that hotels operate on the European Plan (EP, with no meals) unless we specify that they use the Continental Plan (CP, with a Continental breakfast daily) or the Breakfast Plan (BP, with a full breakfast daily).

The lodgings we list are the cream of the crop in each price category. We always list the facilities that are available—but we don't specify whether they cost extra: when pricing accommodations, always ask what's included and what costs extra. Price categories are based on a property's least expensive standard double room at high season (excluding holidays).

CATEGORY	COST*
$$$$	more than R750
$$$	R500–R750
$$	R250–R500
$	less than R250

Rates are for a double room, including VAT.

CITY BOWL

$$$$ **CAPE MILNER HOTEL.** Previously the Mijlhof Manor, this attractive, well-positioned hotel has been extensively refurbished and extended. The new look is clean, classical, and contemporary, with rooms decorated in restful shades of gray, white, and black. The terrace has wonderful views of Table Mountain. *2 Milner Rd., Tamboerskloof, 8001, tel. 021/426–1101, fax 021/426–1109, www. threecities.co.za. 55 rooms, 2 suites. 2 bars, 2 lounges, restaurant, air-conditioning, pool, meeting rooms, parking (fee). AE, DC, MC, V. BP.*

$$$$ **MOUNT NELSON.** This distinctive pink landmark is the grande
★ dame of Cape Town. Since it opened its doors in 1899 to accommodate passengers of the Union-Castle steamships, it has been the focal point of Cape social life. It retains an old-fashioned charm and gentility that other luxury hotels often lack: high tea is served in the lounge to piano accompaniment; the Grill Room offers a nightly dinner dance; and the staff almost outnumbers the guests. The hotel stands at the top of Government Avenue, but, surrounded as it is by 7 acres of manicured gardens, it might as well be in the country. For peak season, December through March, it's advisable to book a year in advance. *76 Orange St., 8001, tel. 021/423–1000, fax 021/424–7472, www.mountnelsonhotel. orient-express.com. 145 rooms, 56 suites. 3 restaurants, bar, 2 pools, gym, 2 tennis courts, squash. AE, DC, MC, V. BP.*

$$$ **BEST WESTERN CAPE SUITES HOTEL.** This is a village-style hotel, with low buildings and adjoining individual units, five minutes from the center of Cape Town, near Parliament, and a 15-minute walk from the waterfront. Rooms are spacious and pleasantly furnished, and all come with a fully equipped kitchen. Some rooms have mountain views; others look into the city. Although it's on a corner site, the hotel is well insulated, so traffic noise is not a major problem; inner rooms tend to be quieter. If you have a car, you can park it virtually outside your room. A free shuttle takes guests to popular sights within about 13 km (8 mi) of the hotel. *Constitution and de Villiers Sts. (Box 51085, Waterfront), 8002, tel. 021/461–0727,*

cape town lodging

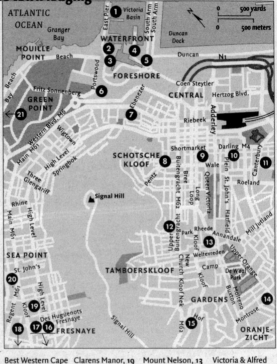

Best Western Cape Suites Hotel, **11**

Breakwater Lodge, **6**

Cape Grace Hotel, **2**

Cape Heritage Hotel, **8**

Cape Milner Hotel, **12**

City Lodge Waterfront, **5**

Clarens Manor, **19**

Cullinan Cape Town Waterfront, **4**

Ellerman House, **18**

Holiday Inn Garden Court– Greenmarket Square, **9**

La Splendida, **21**

Monkey Valley, **17**

Mount Nelson, **13**

No. 7 Hof Street, **15**

Peninsula All Suites Hotel, **20**

Place on the Bay, **16**

Protea Victoria Junction, **7**

Table Bay Hotel, **1**

Townhouse Hotel, **10**

Victoria & Alfred Hotel, **3**

Villa Belmonte, **14**

fax 021/462–4389, www.capesuites.co.za. 126 suites. 2 restaurants, bar, 2 pools, gym, recreation room, free parking. AE, DC, MC, V. EP.

$$–$$$ **VILLA BELMONTE.** In a quiet residential neighborhood on the slopes above the city, this small guest house offers privacy and luxury in an attractive Dutch Revival residence. The owners have sought to create the feeling of an Italian villa through the use of marbling, molded ceilings, and natural wood floors. Wide verandas have superb views of the city, Table Mountain, and Devil's Peak. Rooms have colorful draperies, wicker furniture, and small-pane windows. It's a 20-minute walk to the city center. *33 Belmont Ave., Oranjezicht 8001, tel. 021/462–1576, fax 021/462–1579. 14 rooms. Restaurant, bar, room service, pool. AE, DC, MC, V. BP.*

$$ **CAPE HERITAGE HOTEL.** Friendly, attractive, and well-run, this
★ hotel is part of the Heritage Square development and has direct access to restaurants, shops, and art galleries. Originally built as a private home in 1771, it is now the only black-owned and -managed major hotel in Cape Town. Teak beamed ceilings and foot-wide yellowwood floorboards echo the building's gracious past. Rooms are spacious; some have four-poster beds, others exposed brickwork, but each has its own individual charm. Rooms overlooking the attractive courtyard—where you can find what is said to be the oldest grapevine in South Africa—may be a little noisy, but the revelry stops at midnight sharp. Parking is across the street in a public lot with good security. *90 Bree St., 8001, tel. 021/424–4646, fax 021/424–4949, www.capeheritage.co.za. 14 rooms. Bar, 5 restaurants, breakfast room, 2 lounges, hair salon, shops. AE, DC, MC, V.*

$$ **HOLIDAY INN GARDEN COURT–GREENMARKET SQUARE.** Facing historic Greenmarket Square, this minimum-service hotel has one of the best locations in the city, especially for those who don't have a car. Mountain-facing rooms overlooking the square are pleasant, but the dawn chorus of vendors setting up their stalls may drive you to distraction. The outdoor section of the restaurant, Cycles on the Square, is a popular choice with great views of the market. Parking is a major headache in this part of town. *10 Greenmarket*

Sq. (Box 3775), 8000, tel. 021/423–2040, fax 021/423–3664. 170 rooms. Restaurant, bar. AE, DC, MC, V. EP.

$$ TOWNHOUSE HOTEL. Its proximity to government buildings and its easygoing atmosphere (not to mention extremely competitive rates) make the Townhouse a popular choice. Rooms are decorated in gentle pastels with soft, warm curtains. Request a view of the mountain. 60 Corporation St. (Box 5053), 8000, tel. 021/465–7050, fax 021/465–3891, www.townhouse.co.za. 104 rooms. Restaurant, bar, room service, health club, airport shuttle. AE, DC, MC, V.

$ NO. 7 HOF STREET. If you're staying for a while and have better things to spend your money on than accommodations, this lovely B&B offers excellent value for the money. It's close to everything and within walking distance of the Gardens. The rooms are outside with a separate entrance, and the whole place has a welcoming, homey feel. The rooms are unpretentious, pleasant, clean, and comfortable. One room has a shower and bath, and the other only a bath. 7 Hof St., Gardens 8001, tel. 082/808–3854, tel./fax 021/424–4984. 2 rooms. Breakfast room, pool. No credit cards. CP.

WATERFRONT

$$$$ CAPE GRACE HOTEL. An instant success, this exclusive hotel is
★ on a spit of land jutting into a working harbor. The large guest rooms have harbor or mountain views. The Cape Grace is elegant and understated with French period furnishings and a modern design. It's owned and run by one of the country's leading hotelier families, the Brands. The attention to detail throughout is outstanding, from the antique pieces to the fresh flowers in the rooms. There's a well-stocked library for browsing and a superb restaurant, Quay West (☞ Eating Out). Guests have free use of the nearby health club and the hotel's courtesy car for service into the city. Book well in advance. West Quay, V&A Waterfront, 8002, tel. 021/410–7100, fax 021/419–7622, www.capegrace.com. 122 rooms. Restaurant, bar, pool, library. AE, DC, MC, V. EP.

$$$$ CULLINAN CAPE TOWN WATERFRONT. Just opposite the entrance to the waterfront, this sparklingly white hotel has a spacious marble-tile lobby and huge picture windows draped in rose and gold that lead out to the pool. An enormous double-curving gilt staircase completes the picture. The rooms are quite restrained, with muted green carpets and floral notes; bathrooms are well laid out with separate showers and are quiet and understated in white tile and gray marble. *1 Cullinan St., V&A Waterfront, 8001, tel. 021/418–6920, fax 021/418–3559, www.southernsun.com. 416 rooms. Restaurant, bar, room service, pool, health club. AE, DC, MC, V. EP.*

$$$$ PROTEA VICTORIA JUNCTION. If you're looking for something different, try this funky art deco–style hotel adjacent to the waterfront. The spacious loft rooms have high ceilings and beds on special platforms, but be warned: You have to be nimble to climb to your large double bed in the upstairs section of the room. Standard rooms have ordinary knee-level beds but are still quite chic. The Set is a trendy restaurant for business lunches and has a great range of salads and quite innovative fare, and the bar always jumps at happy hour. *Somerset and Ebenezer Rds., Greenpoint (Box 51234, Waterfront), 8002, tel. 021/418–1234, fax 021/418–5678, www.proteahotels.com. 172 rooms. Restaurant, coffee shop, bar, pool. AE, DC, MC, V.*

$$$$ TABLE BAY HOTEL. In a prime spot at the tip of the V&A Waterfront, this glitzy hotel is sunny and eclectic, with picture windows, marble mosaic and parquet floors, and lots of plants. The hotel's trademark orchid arrangements are made up of more than 1,000 blooms. In the lounge you can browse through the selection of international newspapers as you relax fireside to live chamber music. The understated rooms are colorful and bright, with marble-and-tile bathrooms with roomy showers. Service can be frustratingly inattentive at times. The hotel has direct access to the large Waterfront mall. *Quay 6, V&A Waterfront, 8002, tel. 021/406–5000, fax 021/406–5767, www.suninternational.com. 239 rooms, 15 suites. 3 restaurants, 2 bars, lobby lounge, pool, hair salon, spa, health club, business services, meeting room. AE, DC, MC, V. BP.*

$$$$ VICTORIA & ALFRED HOTEL. Smack in the middle of the waterfront, surrounded by shops, bars, and restaurants, is this upmarket hotel in a converted warehouse. Rooms are huge and furnished in neo–Cape Dutch style. Views from the costlier mountain-facing rooms are spectacular, encompassing Table Mountain, the city, and the docks. Waterfront buses leave regularly for the city center, a five-minute ride. *Pierhead (Box 50050), Waterfront, 8002, tel. 021/419–6677, fax 021/419–8955, www. v-and-a.co.za. 68 rooms. Restaurant, bar, room service. AE, DC, MC, V.*

$$$$ DE WATERKANT VILLAGE. An entire little community of houses are for rent along Cape Town's first and only guest street. There are 30 beautifully restored small houses with kitchen facilities and daily housekeeping services that are unusual, trendy, classy, and quite charming. All are near the harbor, as the name implies. *1 Loader St., 8000, tel. 021/422–2721, fax 021/418–6082, www. dewaterkant.com. AE, DC, MC, V.*

$$$ CITY LODGE WATERFRONT. Location is everything at this no-frills chain hotel, a five-minute walk from the waterfront and 10 minutes from the city center. Rooms are standard, decorated with ship prints and blond-wood furniture, and all have TVs and tea/coffeemakers. *Dock and Alfred Drs. (Box 6025, Roggebaai), Waterfront 8012, tel. 021/ 419–9450, fax 021/419–0460, www.citylodge.co.za. 164 rooms. Bar, breakfast room, pool. AE, DC, MC, V. BP.*

$$ BREAKWATER LODGE. You won't find another hotel this close to the waterfront offering rates so low. Built in a converted 19th-century prison on Portswood Ridge, the Breakwater certainly doesn't win any awards for charm or coziness. Its history is quite evident in the long, narrow corridors, which lead to tiny, sparsely furnished cells—er, rooms. Nevertheless rooms are clean and have TVs, phones, and tea/coffeemakers. Ask for a room with a view of Table Mountain. *Portswood Rd., Waterfront, 8001, tel. 021/406– 1911, fax 021/406–1070, www.breakwaterlodge.co.za. 327 rooms, 110 family units without bath. 2 restaurants, bar. AE, DC, MC, V.*

ATLANTIC COAST

$$$$ BAY HOTEL. Of the luxury hotels in and around Cape Town, this beach hotel in Camps Bay is the most relaxed and unpretentious. The three-story structure is across the road from a white-sand beach and is backed by the towering cliffs of the Twelve Apostles. From the raised pool deck guests look out over sea and sand, far from the hurly-burly of Cape Town. Cane furniture, colorful paintings, and attractive peach and sea tones make the rooms bright. Service is excellent, with an emphasis on privacy. Ask for a premier room if you want a sea view. *Victoria Rd. (Box 32021), Camps Bay 8040, tel. 021/438–4444, fax 021/438–4455, www.halcyonhotels.co.za. 76 rooms. Restaurant, bar, room service, pool, no kids under 12. AE, DC, MC, V. EP.*

$$$$ DE OUDEKRAAL HOTEL. The fantastic location of this luxury hotel is a mixed blessing. The only building between Camps Bay and Llandudno, it borders the Cape Peninsula National Park (it was built just before the park's status was proclaimed), which earned criticism from conservationists. It is also uncomfortably close to a historic Muslim *kramat* (holy burial site), which naturally irked the Muslim community. Despite the vociferous objections, here it stands—and it is beautiful. Sea-facing rooms are decorated in shades of blue; those that face the mountains are brown and green. Built on high ground, it has a spectacular sea view, and the busy Victoria Road is totally out of sight beneath you. *Victoria Rd. (Box 32117), Camps Bay 8040, tel. 021/437–9000, fax 021/437–9001, www.deoudekraal.co.za. 48 rooms, 22 suites. Restaurant, bar, pool, meeting room, travel services. AE, DC, MC, V. EP.*

$$$$ ★ ELLERMAN HOUSE. Without a doubt, this is one of the finest hotels in South Africa. Built in 1912 for shipping magnate Sir John Ellerman, the hotel sits high on a hill in Bantry Bay and has stupendous views of the sea. Broad, terraced lawns fronted by elegant balustrades step down the hillside to a sparkling pool. The drawing and living rooms, decorated in Regency style, are elegant yet not forbiddingly formal. Guest rooms have enormous picture windows, high ceilings, and spacious bathrooms. The hotel accommodates only 22 guests, and a highly trained staff caters to their every whim. In the kitchen four chefs prepare whatever you wish. All drinks except wine and champagne are included in the rates. *180 Kloof Rd., Bantry Bay 8001 (Box 515, Sea Point 8060), tel. 021/439–9182, fax 021/434–7257, www.ellerman.co.za. 11 rooms. Restaurant, bar, room service, pool, sauna, gym. AE, DC, MC, V. CP.*

$$$$ PENINSULA ALL SUITES HOTEL. In an 11-story building across the road from the ocean, this exclusive establishment has a variety of suites that sleep four to eight people and have incredible views of the sea. All suites have full kitchens. The larger suites are full of light and air, thanks to picture windows, sliding doors, wide balconies, and white-tile floors. Small studio suites look more like conventional hotel rooms. The hotel is a time-share property, so booking during the busy December holiday could be a problem. *313 Beach Rd., Sea Point 8001 (Box 768, Sea Point 8060), tel. 021/439–8888, fax 021/439–8886, www.peninsula.co.za. 110 suites. Restaurant, bar, room service, 2 pools, sauna, gym. AE, DC, MC, V.*

$$$$ PLACE ON THE BAY. These luxury apartments are on the beachfront in Camps Bay, within easy walking distance of a host of restaurants and bars. Apartments are tasteful, modern affairs that make extensive use of glass. Many units have good sea views from their balconies. If you really want to have it all, take the magnificent penthouse, which occupies the entire top floor and comes with its own swimming pool, for about R15,000 per day. All units have kithcens and daily housekeeping service. *Fairways and Victoria Rds., Camps Bay 8001, tel. 021/438–7060, fax 021/438–2692, www.theplaceonthebay.co.za. 21 apartments. Restaurant, bar, pool. AE, DC, MC, V.*

$$$ CLARENS MANOR. This beautiful guest house is at once invigorating and extremely restful. Original art, antique furniture, and a few African artifacts stand out against the soft sunshine-yellow walls. Upstairs rooms are grand in size and decor, and the downstairs lounges and dining room are comfortable. Forget the sea view—it's nothing compared to the magnificent spectacle of

Lion's Head looming over you as you gaze from the mountain-facing rooms. Meals are served around one huge table and resemble private dinner parties. Sherry and port, laundry service, and airport shuttle are included in the price. There's a two-night minimum on weekends. If driving, enter Clarens Road from High Level Road, not Regent Street, as it is one-way. *35 Clarens Rd., Sea Point, 8060, tel. 021/434–6801, fax 021/434–6845. 7 rooms. Dining room, 2 lounges, pool, laundry service. AE, DC, MC, V. BP.*

$$$ LA SPLENDIDA. Designed to look like a Miami South Beach art deco hotel, this trendy all-suites addition to the Cape Town scene has a great location on Beach Road, Mouille Point. Ask for a sea- or mountain-facing room—both have great views. Well-proportioned rooms are zany, with bright colors and natural fabrics. Cafe Faro, the outstanding hotel restaurant with interesting eclectic cuisine, is a favorite with local yuppies. The V&A Waterfront is a seven-minute walk. You have a choice of executive or penthouse suites (slightly larger and a bit more expensive), but both are comfortable. *121 Beach Rd., Mouille Point, 8001, tel. 021/439–5119, fax 021/439–5112, www.lasplendida.co.za. 22 suites. Restaurant, lap pool. AE, DC, MC, V.*

$$$ MONKEY VALLEY. This secluded hotel is built on stilts, and each
★ of the thatched log cottages lies in an indigenous milk-wood forest overlooking a nature reserve and the white sands of Noordhoek Beach. The wood interiors are attractive and rustic, with cottage-style furniture and fireplaces. Rooms are similarly decorated, and some have pretty Victorian bathrooms. Cottages have two or three bedrooms, fully equipped kitchens, and large balconies. The resort has its own restaurant, and there is a large grocery store 5 km (3 mi) away. This is one of the best places on the peninsula for families and is very popular for small conferences. Owner Judy Sole runs an outstanding establishment and is a character in her own right. *Mountain Rd. (Box 114), Noordhoek 7985, tel. 021/789–1391, fax 021/789–1143. 34 rooms, 17 cottages. Restaurant, bar, pool, playground, convention center. AE, DC, MC, V. BP.*

$$ **WHALE COTTAGE, BAKOVEN.** This light and airy B&B is fantastically positioned about 200 yards from Bakoven Beach and an easy half-mile walk from Camps Bay Beach. The light, bright, breezy rooms are decorated in a marine or nautical theme and have wonderful sea views. If you want privacy, opt for a downstairs room, as all the upstairs ones open on to the same balcony. *50 Victoria Rd., Bakoven, 8005, tel. 021/438–3840, fax 021/ 438–4388. 6 rooms. Breakfast room, pool. AE, DC, MC, V. CP.*

SOUTHERN SUBURBS

$$$$ **CELLARS-HOHENORT COUNTRY HOUSE HOTEL.** It's easy to
★ forget the outside world at this idyllic getaway. On nine acres of gardens on the slopes of Constantiaberg, this luxury hotel commands spectacular views across Constantia Valley to False Bay. The 18th-century cellars of the Klaasenbosch wine estate and the Hohenort manor house form the heart of the hotel. Rooms are large and elegant, furnished in English-country style with brass beds and reproduction antiques. Rooms in the manor house have the best views of the valley. The Presidential Suite sleeps a family of six. Although the hotel lacks the historical significance of the Alphen, it offers a level of luxury and tranquility that its more famous competitor cannot match. *93 Brommersvlei Rd. (Box 270), Constantia 7800, tel. 021/794–2137, fax 021/794–2149, www. cellarshohenort.com. 55 rooms, 1 suite. 2 restaurants, 2 bars, room service, 2 pools, hair salon, tennis court. AE, DC, MC, V. BP.*

$$$$ **CONSTANTIA UITSIG COUNTRY HOTEL.** This 200-acre winery has
★ an enviable setting, backed by the magnificent mountains of the Constantiaberg and overlooking the vineyards of Constantia Valley. Rooms, in whitewashed farm cottages set amid manicured lawns and gardens, are comfortable and inviting. Wicker headboards, timber ceilings, and bright floral patterns add a rustic feeling. The restaurant in the original farmhouse draws diners from all over the Cape. If you value peace and quiet, this is a great place to stay. *Spaanschemat River Rd. (Box 32), Constantia*

cape peninsula lodging

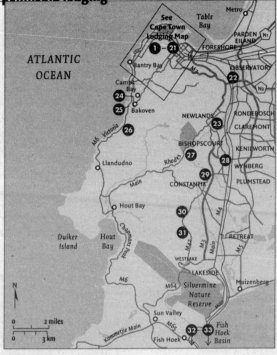

Alphen Hotel, 29

Bay Hotel, 24

Boulders Beach Guesthouse, 33

Cellars-Hohenort Country House Hotel, 27

Constantia Uitsig, 30

De Oudekraal Hotel, 26

Koornhoop Manor Guest House, 22

Quayside Lodge, 32

Palm House, 28

Steenberg Country Hotel, 31

The Vineyard, 23

Whale Cottage, Bakoven, 25

7848, tel. 021/794–6500, fax 021/794–7605, www.constantiauitsig.co.za. 16 rooms. Restaurant, room service, 2 pools. AE, DC, MC, V.

$$$$ STEENBERG COUNTRY HOTEL. The original farm, Swaaneweide aan den Steenberg, was given in the late 17th century to four-time widow Catherina Ustings by her lover, Simon van der Stel, the governor of the Cape. Thus she became the first woman to own land in South Africa. The original buildings have been painstakingly restored, the gardens manicured to perfection, and the vineyards replanted higher up on the mountain. The original vineyards have been converted to a championship 18-hole golf course. The buildings are spectacular and are all furnished with antiques; the rooms are decorated in a Provençal style, with yellow-painted wood and salvaged barn floorboards. *Steenberg and Tokai Rds., Tokai 7945, tel. 021/713–2222, fax 021/713–2221, www.steenberg.com. 23 rooms, 1 suite. Restaurant, bar, 2 pools, hair salon, 18-hole golf course. AE, DC, MC, V. BP.*

$$$$ THE VINEYARD. Set on six acres of rolling gardens overlooking
★ the Liesbeek River in residential Newlands, this comfortable hotel was built around the 18th-century weekend home of Lady Anne Barnard. The lobby is paved in worn terra-cotta tiles and revolves around the leafy breakfast room. The views of the back of Table Mountain are spectacular; the cheaper, courtyard-facing rooms have views of a veritable rain forest growing amid gurgling waters. The hotel is 10 minutes by car from the city but within walking distance of the Newlands sports arenas and the shops of Cavendish Square. Au Jardin (☞ Eating Out), the classic French restaurant, is very well regarded. *Colinton Rd. (Box 151), Newlands 7725, tel. 021/683–3044, fax 021/683–3365, www.vineyard.co.za. 160 rooms. 2 restaurants, bar, room service, pool, gym. AE, DC, MC, V.*

$$$–$$$$ ALPHEN HOTEL. Built between 1750 and 1770 in Cape Dutch style, this former manor house is now a national monument. The owners are descendants of the distinguished Cloete family, which has farmed the land around Constantia since 1750. Cloete paintings and antiques, each with a story to tell, adorn the public rooms.

Rooms range in size from compact to rather large. A small drawback is the slight traffic noise from the nearby highway in rush hour. Only luxury rooms have air-conditioning. *Alphen Dr. (Box 35), Constantia 7848, tel. 021/794–5011, fax 021/794–5710, www.alphen.co.za. 34 rooms. Restaurant, bar, room service, pool. AE, DC, MC, V. BP.*

$$ KOORNHOOP MANOR GUEST HOUSE. One of the best values in Cape Town, this lovely Victorian house in a pretty garden is extremely nice and unpretentious. The rooms, which vary in size, are simply decorated and all have private bath and tea and coffee stations. The hotel is within safe walking distance of a huge range of restaurants in the vibey young suburb of Observatory, a five-minute drive from the city, and convenient to the railway station. A communal TV room with an honor bar is a convivial meeting place. You need to book far in advance to take advantage of this gem. *Wrench and Nuttal Rds., Observatory 7925, tel./fax 021/448–0595, www.geocities.com/koornhoop. 8 rooms, 1 three-bedroom apartment. No credit cards. BP.*

$$ PALM HOUSE. Towering palms dominate the manicured lawns of this peaceful guest house straddling the border of Kenilworth and Wynberg, a 15-minute drive from the city. The house is an enormous, stolid affair, built in the early 1920s by a protégé of Sir Herbert Baker and filled with dark-wood paneling, wood staircases, and fireplaces. Guest rooms are large and decorated reproduction antiques. Upstairs rooms benefit from more air and light. Guests often meet for evening drinks in the drawing room. *10 Oxford St., Wynberg 7800, tel. 021/761–5009, fax 021/761–8776, www.thepalmhouse. co.za. 10 rooms. Bar, pool. AE, DC, MC, V. BP.*

FALSE BAY

$$$ QUAYSIDE LODGE. This limited-service hotel has wonderful views over Simon's Bay, the harbor, and the yacht club. On Jubilee Square, part of the newly built Simonstown Waterfront, it's right in the action. Only five rooms are not sea facing, and all are light and airy, combining lime-washed wood with white walls and pale blue finishes. "Room service" can be arranged from the adjacent Bertha's restaurant or coffee shop. *Jubilee Sq., Main Rd., Simonstown, tel. 021/786–3838, fax 021/786–2241, www.quayside.co.za. 25 rooms, 3 suites. AE, DC, MC, V. BP.*

$–$$ **BOULDERS BEACH GUESTHOUSE.** Positioned just a few steps from the beautiful Boulders Beach—the best swimming beach in Cape Town—this comfortable guest house is a winner. The understated rooms are decorated with elegant black wrought-iron furniture and snow-white linens, creating a restful, minimalist feel. The adjacent restaurant and pub are a bit more boisterous. *4 Boulders Pl., Boulders, Simonstown 7975, tel. 021/786–1758, fax 021/786–1826, www.bouldersbeach.co.za. 13 rooms. Restaurant, bar. AE, DC, MC, V. BP.*

BEYOND THE CAPE PENINSULA

Helderberg (Somerset West)

$$$$ **WILLOWBROOK LODGE.** This lodge lies hidden among beautiful gardens that extend down to the Lourens River. In the distance the peaks of the Helderberg are visible. It's a very peaceful place, with large, airy, comfortable rooms with private bath and sliding doors opening onto the gardens. The cuisine is of an equally high standard, starring Provençal dishes. *Morgenster Ave. (Box 1892) Somerset West 7129, tel. 021/851–3759, fax 021/851–4152. 11 rooms. Restaurant, bar, pool. No children under 12. AE, DC, MC, V. BP.*

Stellenbosch

$$$$ **LANZERAC MANOR.** The sense of history is almost tangible on this large working wine estate dating to 1692. The classic Cape Dutch manor house is flanked by the rolling vineyards and mountains of the Jonkershoek Valley. The luxurious hotel and winery both boast state-of-the-art facilities. Although service is always willing, it does not always live up to opulence of the surroundings. Guest rooms are tastefully decorated. The restaurant

(☞ Side Trips) is excellent. *Jonkershoek Rd. (Box 4) Stellenbosch 7599, tel. 021/887–1132, fax 021/887–2310. 43 rooms, 5 suites. 2 restaurants, bar, room service, pool. AE, DC, MC, V. BP.*

$$$$ **D'OUWE WERF COUNTRY INN.** A national monument, this attractive 1802 inn is thought to be the oldest in South Africa. The hotel is divided into two parts: the old inn with luxury rooms on its Georgian second story and a new wing with more standard rooms. All luxury rooms have antique four-poster beds, draped sash windows, and bronze bathroom fittings. The standard rooms have reproductions only. A lovely coffee garden in a brick courtyard shaded by trellised vines is open for meals and drinks throughout the day. *30 Church St., Stellenbosch 7600, tel. 021/887–1608 or 021/887–4608, fax 021/887–4626. 25 rooms. Restaurant, room service, pool, free parking. AE, DC, MC, V. BP.*

$$$$ **THE VILLAGE AT SPIER.** The innovative design of these two-story buildings grouped around six courtyards, each with its own pool, gives the Village a luxurious Mediterranean feel. Rooms and suites have Indonesian furniture, gas fireplaces, and a wide choice of pillows. Once the surrounding orchards and shade trees have matured, the complex and walkways will be verdant and private. The restaurants here are quite popular. *Spier Estate, Lynedoch Rd., Stellenbosch 7600, tel. 021/809–1100, fax 021/809–1134, www.spier.co.za. 155 rooms. 4 restaurants, bar, room service, pool. AE, DC, MC, V.*

Franschhoek and the Franschhoek Valley

$$–$$$ **LE BALLON ROUGE.** Small but pretty rooms all open onto the wraparound veranda of this early village homestead. The guest house is popular throughout the year with city visitors. The restaurant (☞ Side Trip: The Winelands) attracts nonresidents for lunch and dinner. *7 Reservoir St. (Box 344) Franschhoek 7690, tel. 021/876–2651, fax 021/876–3743. 8 rooms. Restaurant, room service, pool. AE, DC, MC, V. BP.*

$$$$ LE QUARTIER FRANÇAIS. In the center of town, this classy inn is a Winelands favorite. Separated from the village's main drag by a courtyard bistro and a superb restaurant (☞ Side Trips) above, the guest house exudes privacy and peace. Rooms in two-story whitewashed cottages face a pool deck and central garden exploding with flowers. Decor is vibrant, with rustic furniture, sponge-painted walls, colorful drapes, and small fireplaces. Upstairs rooms have timber beams and mountain views, and suites have private pools. *Huguenot Rd. (Box 237) Franschhoek 7690, tel. 021/876-2248 or 021/ 876-2151, fax 021/876-3105, www.lequartier.co.za. 15 rooms, 2 suites. Restaurant, bar, pool. AE, DC, MC, V.*

Paarl

$$$$ BARTHOLOMEUS KLIP FARMHOUSE. For a break from a long bout of wine tasting, head to this Victorian guest house near Wellington on a nature reserve and working farm. Its luxurious accommodations and excellent food come in the middle of 9,900 acres of rare *renosterveld* scrubland that is home to the endangered geometric tortoise. There are also plenty of eland, zebra, wildebeest, springbok, rhebok, bontebok, bat-eared fox, Cape buffalo, and bird life in and around the mountains, streams, and plains. You can hike, mountain bike, or swim here. Rates are all-inclusive. *Bo Hermon Rd., 28 km west of R44 between Wellington and Tulbagh (Box 36) Hermon, 7308, tel. 022/448-1820, fax 022/448-1829, www.parksgroup.co.za. 5 rooms, 1 suite. AE, DC, MC, V.*

$$$$ GRANDE ROCHE. Perhaps the best hotel in South Africa, the
★ Grande Roche is in a gorgeous mid-18th-century Cape Dutch manor house amid acres of vines beneath Paarl Mountain, overlooking the valley and the Drakenstein Mountains. Suites are either in the historic buildings—slave quarters, stables, and wine cellar—or in traditional Cape Dutch–style buildings. In rooms, reed ceilings and thatch comfortably coexist with heated towel racks and air-conditioning. The staff outnumber the guests two to one and offer a level of service extremely rare in South Africa.

Plantasie St. (Box 6038) Paarl 7622, tel. 021/863–2727, fax 021/863–2220, www.granderoche.co.za. 5 rooms, 30 suites. Restaurant, bar, room service, 2 pools, 2 tennis courts, gym. AE, DC, MC, V. BP. Closed June–Aug.

$$$$ **ROGGELAND COUNTRY HOUSE.** In Dal Josaphat Valley, this 1693
★   farm is breathtaking, with stunning views of the craggy Drakenstein
    Mountains. Guest rooms in restored farm buildings have reed
    ceilings and mosquito nets (not just for effect). The 1779 manor
    house, with the dining room and lounge, is a masterpiece of Cape
    Dutch architecture. Dinner and breakfast in the fine restaurant are
    included in the rates. Roggeland Rd., Box 7210, Northern Paarl 7623,
    tel. 021/868–2501, fax 021/868–2113, www.exploreafrica.com/roggeland.
    10 rooms. Restaurant. AE, DC, MC, V. MAP.

In This Chapter

By Andrew Barbour

Updated by Jennifer Stern and Myrna Robbins

side trip:
the winelands

THE WEEKEND PLAYGROUND FOR CAPETONIANS is the Western Cape, and the Winelands are the jewel of the province. Frank Prial, wine critic for the *New York Times*, wrote that he harbored "a nagging suspicion that great wines must be made in spectacular surroundings." If that's true, the French may as well rip up their vines and brew beer, because the Cape Winelands are absolutely stunning. They are a collection of jagged mountains, vine-covered slopes, and centuries-old Cape Dutch estates that produce some of the world's finest wine.

All of this lies only 45 minutes east of Cape Town in three historic towns and valleys. You need a car to get to these wine estates unless you are taking an organized tour. (For information on Winelands tours, *see* Tours in the Practical Information chapter.)

It's no longer entirely accurate to describe these three valleys as *the* Winelands. Today they make up only 35% of all the land in the Cape under vine. This wine-growing region is now so vast you can trek to the fringes of the Karoo Desert, in northeast South Africa, and still find a grape. There are altogether more than 10 wine routes, as well as an established brandy route, in the Western Cape. We have included four here.

The secret to enjoying the Winelands is not to rush. For a day trip, choose only one of the routes listed here and don't push yourself to explore more than two or three wineries.

the winelands

10 miles

10 km

Nelson's Creek **29**

Rheboksloof **28**

Paarl Mountain Nature Reserve

Paarl

R312

R44

R304

Landskroon **27** **30** KWV
26 **31**
Fairview

Afrikaans Language Monument

Glen Carlou

Warwick

Backsberg

Wemmershoek Dam

Villiera **14**

Kraaifontein

12 **25**

24

R45

R303

Simonsig **13**

11 Kanonkop

10 Muratie **19** Plaisir de Merle

La Motte Estate

21

Morgenhof

9

Franschhoek

Jordan Vineyards

15 Thelema

20 L'Ormarins

8

Rustenberg Estate

17 **18** Boschendal

Cabrière **22**

23

Overgaauw **7**

16 Delaire

Helshoogte Pass

La Petite Ferme

Neethlingshof **6**

Stellenbosch

Brug River

R310

Spier **3**

WR7

Assegaaibos Dam

4

R310

STELLENBOSCHBERG

Hottentots Holland Nature Reserve

Theewaterskloof Dam

5 Rust-en-Vrede

R44

FRANSCHHOEK MTNS

Dombeya Farm

R102

R321

R45

Somerset West

Strand

R44

False Bay

Gordon's Bay

2

Elgin

R44

Steenbras Dam

R43

Vergelegen **1**

Morgenster **2**

HELDERBERG (SOMERSET WEST)
40 km (25 mi) southeast of Cape Town on the N2.

Helderberg is the official designation for the wine area referred to as Somerset West. Just before you reach the center of town you'll see the turnoff to Lourensford Road, which runs 3 km (2 mi) to Vergelegen and Morgenster.

★ ❶ **VERGELEGEN.** Established in 1700 by Willem Adriaan van der Stel, who succeeded his father as governor of the Cape, this classic Cape Dutch homestead looks like something out of a fairy tale. An octagonal walled garden aflame with flowers surrounds it, and huge camphor trees, planted almost 300 years ago, stand as gnarled sentinels. The estate was purchased for Lady Phillips by her husband, Sir Lionel, in 1917, and she spent vast sums on its restoration. The homestead is now a museum. Behind the house, Lady Phillips Tea Garden serves lunch and tea, and the Rose Terrace café looks onto a rose garden.

Although Vergelegen still buys grapes from neighboring farms, the vineyards that were planted in 1989 are beginning to give an inkling of some very good wines to come. Taste the flagship Vergelegen, a Bordeaux-style blend, or the merlot, with its ripe, plummy flavors. The chardonnay has touches of wood fermentation but is dominated by a fresh citrus nose. Guided tours are available by appointment and on Saturday and Tuesday at 8:30 AM. Cellar tours are offered from Monday to Saturday at 10:30, 11:30, and 2:30, and reservations are essential. There are no tours in the winter. *Lourensford Rd., Somerset West, tel. 021/847–1334, www.vergelegen.co.za. R7.50. Daily 9:30–4:30 (no tastings Sun. in winter).*

❷ **MORGENSTER.** Just before you reach Vergelegen, take the turnoff to Morgenster. This historic estate has been restored and is now producing wines. Look out for the Lourens River cabernet/merlot blend, which shows promise. They also bottle their own olives and make olive oil and olive pasta. *Box 1616, Somerset West 7129, tel. 021/852–1738. Free. Tasting and sales by appointment only.*

❸ SPIER. Describing this place as simply a wine estate is doing Spier Home Farms an enormous disservice. The vast complex comprises a manor house, wine cellars, wine and farm shop, rose garden, restaurants, conference center, open-air amphitheater, cheetah park, and equestrian facilities. It's all designed in Cape-country style, with whitewashed walls and thatched roofs, set along the verdant north bank of the Eerste River. You can even get to Spier's own little railway station by vintage train from Cape Town. It's seriously touristy, but still delightful. In 2001 the original Spier label was resurrected, replacing the Three Spears label. Try the cabernet sauvignon or the consistently brilliant and well priced chardonnay— there's not a bottle to be found of the previous vintages, but see what the future brings. *R310, Stellenbosch, tel. 021/809–1143, fax 021/881–3634. Free, tastings R10, train ride R75. Daily 9–5.*

❹ RUST-EN-VREDE. Nestled against the base of the Helderberg and shaded by giant oaks, this peaceful winery looks over steep slopes of vines and roses. Owned by former Springbok rugby great Jannie Engelbrecht, it's a comparatively small estate that produces some of the best red wine in South Africa. Rust-en-Vrede Estate is the flagship wine, a blend of predominantly cabernet sauvignon, shiraz, and just over 10% merlot grapes. It has won several awards both locally and abroad, but it would do well to mature in the bottle for another 10 years or more. Another interesting wine is the shiraz, which has an inviting, spicy bouquet with a mellowness imparted by the American oak in which it is matured, but none of the characteristic cloying sweetness; it will age from five to eight years. *R44, between Stellenbosch and Somerset West, tel. 021/881–3881, www.rustenvrede.com. Free. Weekdays 9–5, Sat. 9–4 (Oct.–Apr.) and 9–3 (May–Sept.). Cellar tours on request.*

❺ DOMBEYA FARM. Next door to Rust-en-Vrede winery, this farm is one of the few places in the Western Cape to see spinning and hand weaving. The farm makes jerseys, blankets, and rugs from merino wool, all in the bright, floral patterns that are Dombeya's hallmark. The shop also sells knitting patterns and wool. A garden tearoom serves light lunches and snacks. *Annandale Rd., Stellenbosch, tel./fax 021/881-3746. Daily 9-5.*

Dining

For a description of price categories, *see* the Eating Out chapter.

$$$$ L'AUBERGE DU PAYSAN. South African game birds and venison are used in southern and classic French cuisine at this formal cottage restaurant. Tall upholstered chairs and brass table lamps create a Gallic setting. Start with bouillabaisse or frogs' legs panfried in an herb and garlic butter. Fish entrées could include fresh *kabeljou* topped with sherried cream and grapes. Guinea fowl is used in the cassoulet. Seasonal berries are used in the irresistible desserts. Expect a leisurely meal. *Raithby Rd., off R45, between Somerset West and Stellenbosch, tel. 021/842-2008. AE, DC, MC, V. Closed Sun. and 1 month in winter. No lunch Mon.*

$$$-$$$$ 96 WINERY ROAD. Always buzzing with folk from the wine industry, regulars, and upcountry visitors, this restaurant is relaxed and rustic, with farm implements adorning the walls. Terrace seating offers mountain views. Fresh and flavorful items include a first course of salmon and line-fish sashimi on shredded cucumber and an entrée of butternut, sun-dried tomato, and feta parcels on creamed spinach with pine nuts. Dry-aged cuts of prime beef are grilled and teamed with sauces. A good cheese board is a savory alternative to rich desserts. *Zandberg Farm, Winery Rd., between Somerset West and Stellenbosch, tel. 021/842-2020. Reservations essential. AE, DC, MC, V. No dinner Sun.*

$$$ LADY PHILLIPS RESTAURANT. Reserve a table three weeks in advance in summer at this idyllic country restaurant. Whether dining inside or alfresco in the shade of three-century-old camphor trees, you savor a luncheon of classy simplicity, presented with panache. Appetizers include baked Camembert on *ciabatta* with gooseberry chutney. A grilled beef fillet is served with wild mushrooms and port-wine-marinated onions and the renowned savory pies are always popular. Save room for dessert. If you can't get a reservation, the Rose Terrace café has light meals in summer. *Vergelegen Estate, Lourensford Rd., Somerset West, tel. 021/847–1334. Reservations essential. AE, DC, MC, V. No dinner.*

$$ LA MASSERIA. Plum orchards surround this former dairy farm, now a rustic Italian eatery. Large families tend to arrive early for authentic meals served at long tables. Tuck into the delectable range of antipasti: marinated vegetables, cold meats, and wonderful homemade cheeses and breads. The buffet is R70; additional items cost extra. If gnocchi in burnt sage butter is one of the homemade pastas of the day, don't hesitate. You can bring your own wine, but the house grappa, made from the plums at hand, is good. Cheeses and dried pasta are available to take home. Get good directions. *Stellenrust Estate, Blaauwklippen Rd., Stellenbosch, tel. 021/880–0266. Reservations essential. AE, DC, MC, V. No lunch Mon. No dinner Sun.–Thurs.*

Golf

SOMERSET WEST GOLF CLUB (Rue de Jacqueline, tel. 021/852–2925, fax 021/852–5879) is an easy course (R140 for 18 holes) with plenty of leeway for errant tee shots. **ERINVALE GOLF CLUB** (Lourensford Rd., Somerset West, tel. 021/847–1144) is a Gary Player–designed course (R360 for 18 holes) nestled beneath the Hottentots Holland Mountains.

STELLENBOSCH

★ 15 km (9½ mi) north of Somerset West.

Small, sophisticated, and beautiful, Stellenbosch may be the most delightful town in South Africa. The second-oldest town after Cape Town, it actually *feels* old, unlike many other historic towns in South Africa. The town was founded in 1679 by Simon van der Stel, first governor of the Cape, who recognized the agricultural potential of this fertile valley. Wheat was the major crop grown by the early settlers, but vineyards now blanket the surrounding hills. The town is also home to the University of Stellenbosch, the country's first and most prestigious Afrikaner university. You can walk to all of the sights in the town.

From Stellenbosch, wine routes fan out like spokes of a wheel. You could head west and south along the R310 and R306 toward Spier, Neethlingshof, Overgaauw, and Jordan toward Cape Town. (However, it's not a good route for returning to Cape Town as it gets a bit confusing.) If you head northwest along the R304 toward Simonsig and Villiera or north along the R44 to Morgenhof, Muratie, Delheim, Kanonkop, and Warwick, you'll hit the N1 and can continue to Paarl. Or you could head east on the R310, detouring to Rustenberg and then over the scenic Helshoogte Pass to Thelema Mountain Vineyard, Delaire, and Boschendal, after which you can decide to head right to Franschhoek or left to Paarl.

Stellenbosch is considered to be the center of the Winelands, and many of the older and more established wineries are here. Also based in the town is **DISTELL**, an amalgamation of Stellenbosch Farmers' Winery (SFW) and Distiller's Corporation—two of the biggest producers and distributors in South Africa. SFW is responsible for almost 40% of the country's table wine. The SFW flagship is the Zonnebloem range of reds and whites, including among others a good shiraz (particularly those from the early 1980s). The Lanzerac pinotage was the first of the variety ever made in South Africa (back in 1961), and it's still a good wine.

⑥ NEETHLINGSHOF. A long avenue of pines and oaks leads to this lovely 1692 estate. The magnificent 1814 Cape Dutch manor house looks out across rose gardens to the Stellenbosch Valley and the Hottentots Holland Mountains. The wines produced on this estate and those from its sister farm, Stellenzicht, are highly regarded both locally and abroad, and so be prepared for a rush of tour buses during the high season. The gewürztraminer is an off-dry, very elegant wine with rose-petal and spice aromas, while the Weisser Riesling Noble Late Harvest is one of the best of its kind, having scooped almost every local award since 1990. An unfortunate accident resulted in no 1999 or 2000 vintages. Another fantastic wine from this successful cellar is the almost iconic Stellenzicht Syrah. But you'll have to take it on faith—it's not available for tasting. Three bottles of Stellenzicht is the most they'll sell to one person. R310, tel. 021/883–8988. Free, R20 for 6 tastings. Weekdays 9–5, weekends 10–4. Cellar tours by appointment (stays open 2 hrs later in summer).

⑦ OVERGAAUW. Admire the pretty Victorian tasting room while exploring the range of big proud red wines. Overgaauw was the first South African estate to make a merlot in 1982, and it's still up there with the leaders. It needs a few years to settle, so that the delicious berry nose is able to stand up to the mint/eucalyptus overtones. The Tria Corda is a peppery, minty earthy wine with loads of fruit and oak. The spicy, fruity Sylvaner is the only one in the Cape to date. Stellenbosch Kloof Rd., Vlottenberg, tel. 021/ 881–3815. Free. Weekdays 9–12:30 and 2–5, Sat. 10–12:30.

⑧ JORDAN VINEYARDS. Flanked by the Bottelary hills and overlooking a vision of rolling vineyards and jagged mountains, this fairly new winery enjoys an enviable setting at the head of Stellenbosch Kloof. Gary and Cathy Jordan are a husband-and-wife team who studied at the University of California at Davis and worked at California's Iron Horse Winery. They produced their first vintage in 1992, and have already established a reputation for quality wines. The sauvignon blanc has hints of asparagus and chalky undertones, and the dense but fruity chardonnay is quite popular. Look for a combination of the two in the flavorful and well-priced Chameleon dry white. Wine critics are keeping their eyes on the Jordans' spicy cabernet sauvignon, and the merlot shows great promise. End of Stellenbosch Kloof Rd., tel. 021/881–3441.

Tastings R10. Nov.–Apr. weekdays 10–4:30, Sat. 9:30–2:30; May–Oct. weekdays 10–4:30, Sat. 9:30–12:30. Cellar tours by appointment.

⑨ MORGENHOF. In the lee of a steep hill covered with vines and great pine trees, this winery is on a beautiful 300-year-old Cape Dutch estate. In 1993 it was acquired by the Cointreau-Huchons of Cognac, France. They have spared nothing to make this one of the jewels of the Winelands, and behind the glamour there are an extremely talented wine maker and distinguished wines. Jean Daneel, who made his mark with his award-winning 1992 merlot and his Morgenhof chenin blanc, has moved on, but his student, Rianie Strydom, is carrying on the tradition. Also try the chardonnay with fresh coconut nose and hints of lime, or the smoky, somewhat Burgundian pinotage. A new release is the cabernet sauvignon reserve, a deep, complex wine with hints of tobacco, mint, and ripe plums. From October through April you can reserve picnic baskets and dine on the lawns. The rest of the year there are light lunches of homemade soup, freshly baked bread, cheese, and quiche. Reservations are advisable in summer. *R44, between Paarl and Stellenbosch, tel. 021/889–5510, www.morgenhof.com. Tastings R10. May–Oct. weekdays 9–4:30, weekends 10–3; Nov.–Apr. Mon.–Thurs. 9–5:30, Fri. 9–5, weekends 10–5. Cellar tours by appointment.*

⑩ MURATIE. More concerned with the business of making wine than with decor, Muratie is a refreshing change from "prettier" wineries. It's a small estate, specializing in rich, earthy reds and full-bodied dessert wines. The port is an old favorite in the Cape, and the well-balanced amber is a fortified dessert wine with pleasing citrus overtones to ameliorate the sweetness. The cellar produces two red wines: a pinot noir, from some of the oldest vines of this cultivar in the Cape, and Ansela van der Caab, a dry red blend of cabernet and merlot, named after the freed slave who married the first owner of the farm and helped set up the vineyards. *Knorhoek Rd., Koelenhof, tel. 021/882–2330. Free. Apr.–Oct. weekdays 10–5, Sat. 10–3; Nov.–Mar. weekdays 10–5, Sat. 10–3, Sun. 11–3. Cellar tours by appointment only.*

⑪ KANONKOP. In the days when ships of the Dutch East India Company used Cape Town as a revictualing station on the way to the East, a ship would fire a cannon as it entered the harbor to let farmers know provisions were needed. Then a set of relay cannons, all set on hilltops, would carry the message far inland. One such cannon was on this farm, which was then called Kanonkop, which is Afrikaans for Cannon Hill. The beauty is not in its buildings but in its wine. Since the early 1980s wine making has been in the hands of legendary Beyers Truter. In 1991 he won the Winemaker of the Year award and the Robert Mondavi Trophy at the International Wine & Spirit Competition in London. Few would argue that Kanonkop's pinotage is the best new-style pinotage in South Africa. It's more wooded than most and shows excellent complexity and fruit; it ages in 8 to 15 years. Paul Sauer is a very good blend of 80% cabernet sauvignon with equal parts merlot and cabernet franc. The 1995 vintage won a gold medal at the 1998 International Wine & Spirit Competition. No cellar tours are offered. *R44, between Paarl and Stellenbosch, tel. 021/884–4656. Tastings free. Weekdays 8:30–5:30, Sat. 8:30–12:30.*

⑫ WARWICK. Visit this estate only if you're very keen to taste and buy wine; the tasting area is in a tiny cellar room cluttered with wine-making equipment (if possible, make an appointment first). The previous wine maker, Norma Ratcliffe, spent a couple of vintages in France perfecting her rather traditional techniques, which have left their mark on Warwick's reds. Trilogy is one of the finest blended reds in the Cape, a stylish and complex wine made predominantly from cabernet sauvignon, with about 40% merlot and 7% cabernet franc. The cabernet franc is undoubtedly one of the best wines made from this varietal in the Winelands. The new wine maker, Anna-Marie Mostert, has a hard act to follow, but she proved her worth at Mont Rochelle in Franschhoek. *R44, between Paarl and Stellenbosch, tel. 021/884–4020, fax 021/884–4025. Tastings R5. Weekdays 8:30–4:30, Sat. by appointment. Cellar tours by appointment.*

🐌 ⓭ **SIMONSIG.** The views of Stellenbosch and the mountains are tremendous at this estate. Its range of 15 white and red wines covers the taste and price spectrum. Kaapse Vonkel was South Africa's first Méthode Cap Classique sparkling wine and, 30 years on, is still among the best with 15% pinotage, 50% chardonnay, and 35% pinot. Tiara is among the best cabernet blends in the Winelands, and the pinotage is an excellent example of how well this varietal fares with no wood aging—but the Pinotage Red Hill, from old bush vines, shows just how much good oaking can improve it. You can bring your own picnic to enjoy at tables by the small playground. *Kromme Rhee Rd., tel. 021/882–2044, fax 021/882–2545, www.simonsig.co.za. Tastings R5. Weekdays 8:30–5, Sat. 8:30–4. Cellar tours weekdays at 10 and 3, Sat. at 10.*

★ ⓮ **VILLIERA.** Actually part of the Paarl Wine Route, Villiera's location in the open flats near the N1 motorway makes it just as close to Stellenbosch as to Paarl. The Grier family has been making wine for over 15 years. As John Platter, one of South Africa's foremost wine writers, says: "Other wine makers might jog or work out in the gym; Jeff Grier gets all the exercise he needs stepping up to the podium for wine industry awards." Try the Bush Vine Sauvignon Blanc, for which Grier was voted Winemaker of the Year, and you might understand why it's become almost a cult wine. Check out the range of Cap Classique sparkling wines. The Tradition rosé brut, made from pinot, chardonnay, and 10% pinotage, is a delicate pink bubbly with soft, creamy overtones. This winery strives to produce chemical-free wines. *R101 and R304 (Old Paarl and Stellenbosch Rds.), Koelenhof, tel. 021/882–2002. Tastings free. Weekdays 8:30–5, Sat. 8:30–1. Guided tours by appointment only.*

⓯ **RUSTENBERG ESTATE.** Dating from 1682, this estate is now a state-of-the art winery with underground vaulted maturation rooms. The estate is known for red wine, particularly its 100% cabernet Peter Barlow (named after the owner's father). It's made from grapes of one lovely, well-tended vineyard that unfortunately suffered extensive damage in the fires of 2000; the deep red 1999

vintage will be the last for a while. It's a lovely unblended wine
that ages for a decade or two. Snap up a few bottles if you can.
From Idasvallei Road, follow a narrow lane, which runs through
cattle pastures and oak groves to the estate. *Idasvallei Rd., off
R310 (Rustenberg Rd.), Ida's Valley, tel. 021/809–1200, www.rustenberg.
co.za. Tastings free. Weekdays 9–4:30, Sat. 9–12:30 Cellar tours by
appointment.*

16 DELAIRE. Sit on the terrace of the tasting room or restaurant at
this winery, and look past the oaks to the valley below and the
majestic crags of the Groot Drakenstein and Simonsberg
mountains. The restaurant (open from Tuesday to Saturday noon–
2) serves light lunches and provides picnic baskets if you want
to follow one of the scenic trails through the estate (September
15–April 15). The tasting room is unpretentious and casual. The
winery has two labels; Botmaskop (try the cabernet sauvignon
or the flagship merlot) and the alternative Green Door range,
named after the winery restaurant. There are no cellar tours.
*R310, between Stellenbosch and Franschhoek (Helshoogte Rd.), tel. 021/
885–1756, www.delaire.co.za. Tastings R10, R12 glass deposit. Mon.–
Sat. 10–5.*

17 THELEMA MOUNTAIN VINEYARDS. When Gyles and Barbara
Webb bought a farm on the slopes of Simonsberg in 1983, there
was nothing here but very good soil and old fruit trees. The winery
has had regular prizewinners ever since. The 1992 cabernet
sauvignon–merlot blend won Gyles Webb the Diner's Club
Winemaker of the Year title in 1994. Two years later he took the
award again with the '94 cabernet. The whites are nothing to sneer
at either: Thelema's sauvignon blanc and chardonnay are certainly
among the Cape's best. The view of the Groot Drakenstein
Mountains from the tasting room is unforgettable. This vineyard
suffered severe damage from the fires of 2000 and will have a
decreased output as a result. *R310, between Stellenbosch and
Franschhoek (Helshoogte Pass), tel. 021/885–1924. Tastings free.
Weekdays 9–5, Sat. 9–1.*

Dining

$$$$ GOVERNOR'S RESTAURANT AT LANZERAC MANOR. The classic Cape Dutch manor house on this 1692 estate is flanked by rolling vineyards and mountains of the Jonkershoek Valley. The restaurant has a Cape Malay and cheese buffet at lunchtime, upholding a popular tradition dating back decades. Dinner entrées include loin of lamb filled with avocado and accompanied by oyster mushrooms, herbed mashed potatoes, and yellow tomato sauce or wild boar on gazpacho with potato gnocchi. *Jonkershoek Rd., 1 km (½ mi) from Stellenbosch, tel. 021/887–1132. AE, DC, MC, V.*

$$$$ JONKERSHUIS AT SPIER. Cape Malay, Dutch, French, and German cuisines are celebrated here with a R120-per-head buffet feast that you can savor under venerable oaks or in the well-restored 18th-century homestead. Start with local seafood dishes such as *snoek* pâté or excellent pickled fish. Hearty entrées include Cape chicken pie, *bredie* (lamb casserole in a tomato sauce), and Malay curries. Look for the time-honored desserts like *melktert* (a sweet custard tart sprinkled with cinnamon and sugar). *Spier Estate, Lynedoch Rd., tel. 021/809–1172. AE, DC, MC, V. No dinner Sun. and Mon.*

Outdoor Activities

GOLF
STELLENBOSCH GOLF CLUB (Strand Rd., tel. 021/880–0103) has long tree-lined fairways that pose a problem if you don't hit the ball straight. Greens fees are R200 for 18 holes.

HORSEBACK RIDING
At the **SPIER EQUESTRIAN CENTRE** (tel. 083/627–2282) you can gently amble or quickly canter through the vineyards (R80 per hour). You can also do a tasting with your trusty mount standing by. Horse-drawn wagon rides are R40 per person for half an hour, and R80 for an hour.

FRANSCHHOEK AND THE FRANSCHHOEK VALLEY

22 km (14 mi) northeast of Stellenbosch.

From Thelema the road runs down Helshoogte Pass into the fruit orchards and vines that mark the beginning of the Franschhoek Valley. This is the most isolated and spectacular of the three wine routes, a long valley encircled by towering mountain ranges and fed by a single road.

18 BOSCHENDAL. With a history dating back three centuries, this lovely estate competes with Groot Constantia as one of the Cape's major attractions; you could easily spend half a day here. Cradled between the Simonsberg and Groot Drakenstein mountains, the farm was originally granted to Jean le Long, one of the first French Huguenot settlers in the late 17th century. Boschendal runs one of the most pleasant wine tastings in the region: You can sit inside at the Taphuis, a Cape Dutch longhouse and the oldest building on the estate, or outside at wrought-iron tables under a spreading oak. In 1980 Boschendal was the first to pioneer a Cape blanc de noir, a pink wine made in a white-wine style from black grapes. The Boschendal Blanc de Noir remains the best-selling wine of this style. The extremely popular Boschendal Brut is a blend of pinot noir and chardonnay made by the Méthode Cap Classique. From the Taphuis it's a two-minute drive through vines and fruit trees to the main estate complex. The excellent Boschendal Restaurant serves a buffet of Cape specialties. Le Café serves light meals at tables under the oaks leading to the manor house. And Le Pique Nique (open November–April) provides picnic baskets that you can enjoy on the lawns. Calling ahead for the restaurant and the picnic is essential. A gift shop sells wine, locally made rugs, preserves, and other Cape kitsch. The estate is wheelchair-accessible. *R310, between Franschhoek and Stellenbosch (Pniel Rd., Groot Drakenstein), tel. 021/870–4274, www.boschendalwines. co.za. Tastings R5. Dec.–Jan. Mon.–Sat. 8:30–4:30, Sun. 9:30–12:30; May–Oct. weekdays 8:30–4:30, Sat. 8:30–12:30; Nov. and Feb.–Apr.*

Mon.–Sat. 8:30–4:30. Combined cellar and vineyard tours Nov.–Apr. daily 10:30 and 11:30.

⑲ PLAISIR DE MERLE. If you're planning to visit Franschhoek and then return to Paarl, leave Plaisir de Merle for the return trip. This huge estate (2,500 acres) is Distell's showpiece. With its innovative architecture and conservation area, it truly feels different from the rather run-of-the-mill, ubiquitous "oak and gable" wineries that you see all over the Cape. But forget all the frills—it's about the wine. Don't miss the cabernet sauvignon, probably the smoothest, lowest-acid, lowest-tannin local example of this cultivar. *From R310, turn left onto R45, then left again, Simondium, tel. 021/874–171 or 021/874–1072, www.plaisirdemerle.co.za. Weekdays 9–5, Sat. 10–1.*

⑳ L'ORMARINS. Dating back to 1811, this estate's classic Cape Dutch manor house is festooned with flowers and framed by majestic peaks. The huge tasting room is modern, as is the wine-making style. Using classic grape varieties, the wine makers produce big, complex red wines ready for early drinking but with excellent maturation potential. Optima is such a wine. A blend of predominantly cabernet sauvignon and merlot, it has great complexity that will improve in the bottle for 10–15 years. The straight cabernet is just as pleasing; among whites, try the pinot gris. *R45 (Franschhoek Rd.), Groot Drakenstein, tel. 021/874–1026. Tasting by appointment only. Cellar tours weekdays at 10, 11:30, and 3.*

㉑ LA MOTTE ESTATE. Owned by a branch of the same Rupert family that owns L'Ormarins, La Motte has an elegant and rather formal tasting room that looks into the cellars through a wall of smoked glass. You sit at a long marble-top table and sample from five to seven wines. The shiraz is one of the biggest and boldest you'll taste of this variety, full of rich flavors; it needs from four to eight years to reach its peak. The Millennium is a very good blend of just over 50% cabernet sauvignon with the balance consisting of merlot and a little cabernet franc. This wine needs time to develop, coming into its own in 5–10 years. There are no cellar tours. *R45*

(Huguenot Rd.), less than 2 km (1 mi) from the bridge over the Berg River, tel. 021/876–3119, www.la-motte.co.za. Tastings R5. Weekdays 9–4:30, Sat. 9–noon.

㉒ CABRIÈRE. Built in 1994 on the lower slopes of the Franschhoek Mountains, Cabrière is the brainchild of Achim von Arnim, one of the Cape's most colorful wine makers. To avoid scarring the mountain, the complex hunkers into the hillside. There are five Cap Classique sparkling wines under the Pierre Jordan label, while the fruity, mouth-filling Haute Cabrière pinot noir is consistently one of the best. Also delicious is the chardonnay–pinot noir blend, an ideal, extremely quaffable wine to enjoy at lunchtime. Take a Saturday-morning cellar tour with von Arnim, and watch him perform his trademark display of *sabrage*—the dramatic decapitation of a bottle of bubbly with a saber. R45, tel. 021/876–2630, www.cabriere.co.za. Tastings R5, cellar tours and tastings R20. Sales, weekdays 9–1 and 2–4:30, Sat. 11–1; tours Sat. 11 or by appointment.

㉓ LA PETITE FERME. You have to phone ahead to arrange a tasting here, but it's worth it. True to its name, this is a small, family-run estate producing just enough wine for the restaurant and to keep its faithful regular customers happy. Try the chardonnay. R45, Franschhoek, tel. 021/876–3016. Sales daily noon–4, tasting and tours by appointment only.

㉔ BACKSBERG. Framed by the mountains of the Simonsberg, this lovely estate is run by the Back family, well known for producing great wines of good value. An unusual feature is the self-conducted cellar tour. You follow painted lines around the cellars, pausing to watch video monitors that explain the wine-making process. It's a low-pressure introduction to wine making and an ideal starting point for novices. Backsberg produces a comprehensive range of red and white wines, a Méthode Cap Classique sparkling wine, and a very fine brandy made from chenin blanc. The chardonnay is consistently one of the best made, a rounded, fruity wine that develops well in the bottle for five or more years.

Backsberg is one of only a handful of estates that produce a malbec—and then only in very small quantities. The new Freedom Road range is made by a worker–management project—so far it has produced only a sauvignon blanc. *WR1, between R44 and R45 (Simondium Rd.), tel. 021/875–5141, www.backsberg.co.za. Tastings R5, cellar tours free. Weekdays 8:30–5, Sat. 8:30–1.*

㉕ GLEN CARLOU. The cellar is not particularly pretty, but what comes out of it is rather special. As well as fine wines—especially the chardonnay reserve—the winery also produces a range of farm cheeses and olives. Add a loaf of bread, and you've got everything you could possibly want for an impromptu picnic. *Off Simondium Rd., first right after Backsberg, Klapmuts 7625, tel. 021/875–5528, www.glencarlou.co.za. Tastings R5. Weekdays 8:45–4:45, Sat. 9–12:30.*

㉖ FAIRVIEW. This is one of the few wineries where visitors might feel comfortable taking their families. Children get a kick out of peacocks roaming the grounds and goats clambering up a spiral staircase into a goat tower. Every afternoon at four the goats are milked. Fairview produces a superb line of goat cheeses, all of which you can taste gratis. A deli counter sells sausages and cold meats to complement the estate's wines and cheeses. Don't let Fairview's sideshows color your judgment about the wines. Charles Back, a member of the family that runs Backsberg, is one of the most successful and innovative wine makers in the Cape, and the estate's wines are excellent. Certainly, Back does not stick to the tried-and-tested Cape varietals. The zinfandel–cinsaut blend is quite unusual, and they make creative use of the many Rhône varieties planted on the farm. Perhaps it's just because the pun was irresistible, but (as claimed by the label) they send the milk-producing goats into the vineyard to personally select the best grapes, from which they make their very personal Goats-do-Roam. Yes, it is rather like a young Côtes du Rhône. *WR3, off R101 (Suid-Agter-Paarl Rd.), tel. 021/863–2450, www.fairview.co.za. Tastings free. Weekdays 8:30–5, Sat. 8:30–1. Cellar tours by appointment.*

27 **LANDSKROON.** Almost next door to Fairview is this venerable estate now run by the ninth generation of the de Villiers family. They produce a lovely cabernet franc, and their cabernet sauvignon—with hints of vanilla and oak—is up there with the best. After a long, leisurely dinner, try the Murio Muscat Jerepico—a rich, velvety fortified wine with a fresh finish. There is a playground for children and a coffee shop on the terrace. *WR3, off R101 (Suid-Agter-Paarl Rd.), Suider Paarl, tel. 021/863–1039, www.landskroon.co.za. Free. Weekdays 8:30–5, Sat. 9–1.*

Dining

$$$$ **BOSCHENDAL RESTAURANT.** Reserve well in advance for the buffet lunch here at one of the Cape's most beautiful and historic wineries. There's a wide selection of soups, quiches, and pâtés, and hot main dishes include pickled fish, roasts, and imaginative salads. Traditional Cape dishes are well prepared. Service is unobtrusive, professional, and friendly and well complements the bounty. Meals are prix fixe at R125. *R310, between Franschhoek and Stellenbosch, tel. 021/870–4274. Reservations essential. AE, DC, MC, V. No dinner.*

$$$$ **MONNEAUX.** Asian and Western flavors and techniques merge in dishes starring local ingredients, best illustrated in the five-course gastronomic menu. From the à la carte menu, you can start with raw beef marinated in lemongrass or dried shrimp teamed with ruby grapefruit and dried mango with a chili-mint chutney. Spiced red bell pepper flavors the prawn risotto, and the farfalle with roast vegetables, basil pesto, and shaved Parmesan is a hit. At lunch, savor your meal on the shady terrace. You can stay the night in the 19th-century former *parfumerie* and guest house if you reserve in advance. *Main Rd., Franschhoek, tel. 021/876–3386. Reservations essential. AE, DC, MC, V.*

$$$–$$$$ **HAUTE CABRIÈRE.** Dine here atop a working winery built into the mountainside. Try to reserve a window table for views across the vine-clad valley. The mix-and-match menu has been created to

complement the estate wines. Mouthwatering fare changes with the seasons. A basil risotto with oyster mushrooms, red bell pepper, and black olives titillates the palate; follow with fresh Scottish salmon teamed with spinach, potato galette, and horseradish cream. Or choose the local salmon trout or roast rack of Karoo lamb. Belgian-trained chocolatiers contribute to the luscious selection of desserts. *R45, Franschhoek Pass, Franschhoek, tel. 021/876–3688. Reservations essential. AE, DC, MC, V. No dinner Tues.*

$$–$$$$ LE QUARTIER FRANÇAIS. This restaurant in a 19th-century home garners local and international awards. On summer nights glass doors open onto a lighted garden; in winter a log fire burns in the hearth. You might start with mixed wild mushrooms on toasted brioche with Kalahari truffles and wild arugula in autumn. Roasted chicken with sweet-corn pancakes and fillet of veal are popular main courses. Cheese dishes—such as local Camembert with roasted pear and red-wine syrup—make innovative desserts. *16 Huguenot Rd., Franschhoek, tel. 021/876–2151. Reservations essential. AE, DC, MC, V. No dinner Sun.*

$$$ TOPSI & COMPANY. Chef Topsi Venter, doyenne of the Cape culinary scene, is as renowned as a raconteur as she is for her innovative country fare. The menus, written on a blackboard, change daily, and only local and fresh ingredients are used. Entrées vary from a hearty dish of roast pork loin on colcannon, lent piquancy by a dried peach and yellow bell pepper salsa to panfried sirloin of gemsbok (venison) with braised endive. Unconventional desserts include a tart filled with Smyrna dried figs, hazelnuts, and chili, topped with a dollop of bay-leaf-infused cream. Bring your own wine. *7 Reservoir St., Franschhoek, tel. 021/876–2952. Reservations essential. DC, MC, V.*

$$$ LE BALLON ROUGE RESTAURANT. The menu at the restaurant of this early village homestead inn presents a straightforward but substantial choice of well-cooked fare. Black mussels, local smoked salmon trout in pastry, and spring rolls filled with bobotie are among the first courses. Most entrées are priced at R42, including chicken breast in white wine, rainbow trout stuffed with spinach and almond butter, and line fish of the day. *7 Reservoir St., Franschhoek, tel. 021/876–2651. AE, DC, MC, V.*

PAARL

21 km (13 mi) northwest of Franschhoek.

This town takes its name from the granite domes of Paarl Mountain, which looms above the town—*paarl* is Dutch for pearl. The first farmers settled here in 1687, two years after the founding of Stellenbosch. The town has its fair share of historic homes and estates, but it lacks the charm of its distinguished neighbor simply because it's so spread out. Main Street, the town's oak-lined thoroughfare, extends some 11 km (7 mi) along the western bank of the Berg River. You can gain a good sense of the town's history on a drive along this lovely street.

㉘ RHEBOKSKLOOF. The winery sits at the head of a shallow valley, backed by hillsides covered with vines and fynbos. It's a lovely place for lunch on a sunny day. The Victorian Restaurant serves à la carte meals and teas on an oak-shaded terrace overlooking the gardens and mountains; in inclement weather meals are served in the Cape Dutch Restaurant, as is a Sunday buffet lunch. The Chardonnay Sur Lie is the pick of the bunch, with a lovely balance and fruity, toasty overtones. You can also take horse rides through the vineyards. No cellar tours are offered. *WR8, off R44, tel. 021/863–8386, www.rhebokskloof.co.za. Tastings R7. Daily 9–5.*

㉙ NELSON'S CREEK. A huge geological fault runs through the estate, and is partly responsible for the multiple soil types here that result in a profusion of microclimates. But that's just the physical background. In 1997 Alan Nelson, the owner of Nelson's Creek, decided that land redistribution was a good idea, so he gave 11 hectares (24 acres) of prime vineyard to the farmworkers to inaugurate the New Beginnings program. From the proceeds of their first vintage they bought another 9 hectares (20 acres).

Mathewis Thabo, who started off as a part-time gardener on the estate, is now producing three pretty respectable wines—a red, a white, and a rosé. Nelson's Creek, too, produces some fantastic reds. The cabernet sauvignon is a big, ripe blackberry-flavored wine with a hint of spice; the pinotage is unwooded and, although a bit unusual, has been well received. However, the best buy is probably the inexpensive, very drinkable Albenet, a cinsaut/shiraz blend. It's also a great place for a picnic or a walk. Cellar tours are by appointment only. *R44, Paarl, tel. 021/863–8453. Weekdays 8–5, Sat. 9–2.*

③⓪ KO-OPERATIEVE WIJNBOUWERS VERENIGING (KWV). For nearly 80 years the Cooperative Winegrowers' Association has regulated and controlled the Cape wine industry. KWV sells wine and spirits in more than 40 countries and more than 30 U.S. states, and its brandies, sherries, and fortified dessert wines regularly garner gold medals at the International Wine & Spirit Competition in London. It also offers one of the most popular and most crowded cellar tours in the Winelands. Its cellars are the largest in the world, covering some 55 acres. Among the highlights is the famous Cathedral Cellar, with a barrel-vaulted ceiling and giant vats carved with scenes from the history of Cape wine making. In an adjoining cellar you can see under one roof the five largest vats in the world. The tour ends with a tasting. *André du Toit Bldg., Kohler St., tel. 021/807–3007, www.kwv.co.za. Cellar tours and tastings R10. Tours by appointment only; English tours at 11 and 2:15; tastings weekdays 8–4:30, Sat. 8:30–4.*

③① AFRIKAANS LANGUAGE MONUMENT (Afrikaanse Taalmonument). High on a hill overlooking Paarl, this concrete structure holds a special place in the hearts of Afrikaners, who struggled for years to gain acceptance for their language alongside English. The rising curve of the main pillar is supposed to represent the growth and potential of Afrikaans. Ironically, it may become the language's memorial. Under the new South Africa Afrikaans has become just one of 11 official languages and is gradually losing its dominance. The view from the top of the hill is incredible, taking in Table Mountain, False Bay, Paarl Valley, and the various mountain ranges of the Winelands. A short, paved walking trail leads around the hillside past impressive fynbos specimens, particularly proteas. *Afrikaanse Taalmonument Rd., off Main St., follow the sign after the N1 bridge, tel. 021/863–4809. R5. Daily 9–5.*

Dining

$$$$ **BOSMAN'S.** Amid the heady opulence of the Grande Roche hotel,
★ this elegant restaurant ranks as one of the country's finest. The service is commensurate with that of the finest European restaurants, although some may find the attention suffocating. Choose from the seafood, gourmet, Cape flavored, vegetarian, low-fat gourmet, or à la carte menus, all of which change daily. Everyone gets a complimentary *amuse-bouche* (literally, something to entertain your mouth). An à la carte first course of breast of pigeon with creamy leeks and truffle sauces could precede an entrée of roasted tuna with wild mushrooms and bacon foam. Gratinéed pineapple with coconut ice cream wraps up the meal in sophisticated style. *Grand Roche hotel, Plantasie St., tel. 021/863–2727. AE, DC, MC, V. Closed June–Aug.*

$$$$ **ROGGELAND.** For an unforgettable Cape experience, make a beeline for this glorious Cape Dutch manor house on a farm outside Paarl. Meals are long, languid rituals, whether it's an alfresco lunch in the garden or a four-course dinner in the 18th-century dining room. A main course of lamb loin comes teamed with roasted butternut and shallots in muscadel with an indigenous dessert of malva pudding (a baked sponge pudding) with a *rooibos* (a native legume) tea mousse as the finale. This feast is priced at R130 and includes a different wine with each course. *Roggeland Rd., North Paarl, tel. 021/868–2501. Reservations essential. AE, DC, MC, V.*

$$–$$$$ **PONTAC MANOR.** Fast becoming a Winelands favorite, this restaurant is paired with an inn on a former Cape Victorian homestead. The deep veranda is the place for lunch except on hot

days, when the elegant dining room makes a cooler option. A distinct Cape accent is discernible in dishes like duck breast with citrus segments, mango, and bell pepper and venison with polenta accompanied by burnt banana quenelles. To finish, try the cheesecake mille-feuille on an amaretto syrup garnished with chocolate cigars. *Pontac Manor, 16 Zion St., Paarl, tel. 021/872–0445. AE, DC, MC, V.*

Outdoor Activities

BALLOONING
Every morning from about November to March or April, weather permitting, **WINELAND BALLOONING** (tel. 021/863–3192) makes one-hour flights over the Winelands. The balloon holds a maximum of six people, and the trip costs about R1,200 per person. After the flight there's a champagne breakfast.

GOLF
PAARL GOLF CLUB (Wemmershoek Rd., tel. 021/863–1140) is surrounded by mountains, covered with trees, and dotted with water hazards. The greens fee is R170 for 18 holes.

HORSEBACK RIDING
Scenic rides around the vineyards or into the surrounding Paarl Nature Reserve are given at **WINE VALLEY HORSE TRAILS** (tel. 083/226–8735 or 021/863–8687), based at Rhebokskloof winery. A four-hour ride gets you to the far side of the hill, from where you have a distant view of Table Mountain. Prices range from R80 for a one-hour ride to R350 for a full day, including lunch.

practical information

Addresses

Air Travel to and from Cape Town

Cape Town International Airport lies 22½ km (14 mi) southeast of the city in the Cape Flats. The airport is tiny: the domestic and international terminals are no more than 200 yards apart. In addition to a VAT refund office, there is a Western Cape Tourism Board booth with an accommodations hot line, open daily 7–5, that provides information on guest houses around the city. Trust Bank exchanges money weekdays 9–3:30 and Saturday 8:30–10:30; it stays open later for international arrivals and departures.

BOOKING

When you book look for **nonstop flights** and **remember that "direct" flights stop at least once.** Try to avoid connecting flights, which require a change of plane. Two airlines may operate a connecting flight jointly, so ask if your airline operates every segment of the trip; you may find that the carrier you prefer flies you only part of the way. For more booking tips and to check prices and make on-line flight reservations, log on to www.fodors.com.

CARRIERS

International carriers flying into Cape Town include Air Namibia, British Airways, Lufthansa, South African Airways, and Virgin Atlantic. The major domestic carriers serving Cape Town

are British Airways/Comair, Sabena/Nationwide, and South
African Airways, SA Airlink, and SA Express.

➤ **AIRLINES AND CONTACTS: Air Namibia** (tel. 021/936–2755).
British Airways (tel. 086/001–1747). **British Airways/Comair** (tel.
086/001–1747). **Lufthansa** (tel. 086/057–2573, www.lufthansa.
com). **Sabena/Nationwide** (tel. 021/936–2050, www.flynationwide.
com). **South African Airways, SA Airlink,** and **SA Express** (tel. 021/
936–1111, www.flysaa.com). **Virgin Atlantic** (tel. 01293/747–747).

CHECK IN AND BOARDING
For domestic flights, arrive at the airport at least two hours
before your scheduled departure time. For international flights,
plan on arriving at the airport at least 2½ hours before
departure, but be sure to ask your carrier whether it requires an
earlier check-in.

Assuming that not everyone with a ticket will show up, airlines
routinely overbook planes. When everyone does, airlines ask for
volunteers to give up their seats. In return, these volunteers
usually get a certificate for a free flight and are rebooked on the
next flight out. If there are not enough volunteers, the airline
must choose who will be denied boarding. The first to get
bumped are passengers who checked in late and those flying on
discounted tickets, so get to the gate and check in as early as
possible, especially during peak periods.

Always bring a government-issued photo I.D. to the airport;
even when it's not required, a passport is best.

Airports and Transfers
You'll need to call a shuttle from the airport if you'd like one, as
there are no scheduled shuttles from Cape Town Airport. A trip
between the airport and the city center costs between R60 and
R150, depending on direction and number of passengers. Or
travel in comfort in a stretch limo from Cape Limo Services for

about R700 per hour, with a minimum of an hour and a half, or R350–R400 per hour for longer trips.

➤ **AIRPORT INFORMATION: Cape Town International Airport** (tel. 021/934–0407).

➤ **TAXIS AND SHUTTLES: Cape Limo Services** (tel. 021/785–3100). **Gary's Shuttles** (tel. 021/426–1641). **Magic Bus** (tel. 021/510–6001).

Business Hours

Business hours in Cape Town are quite standard, weekdays from about 9 to 5. Most banks close in mid-afternoon, but currency exchange offices usually stay open longer. In addition, post offices and banks are open on Saturday morning from about 9 to noon. Many shopping malls are open until 9 or 10 at night and are open on Sunday.

Bus Travel to and from Cape Town

Greyhound offers daily overnight service to Johannesburg and Pretoria. Intercape Mainliner operates a far more extensive network of routes in the Western Cape than does Greyhound, with daily service up the N7 to Springbok and Windhoek, along the Garden Route to George and Port Elizabeth; a bus also travels daily to Johannesburg. Both Intercape and Greyhound can be booked through Computicket. The Baz Bus offers a service aimed mostly at backpackers who don't want to travel vast distances in one day and don't have transportation to get to train or bus stations. It's a hop-on/hop-off service that is more expensive than the straight bus but so much more convenient— especially if you're planning a long trip in short stages.

FARES AND SCHEDULES

Overnight service one-way to Johannesburg and Pretoria is about R375–R450. Cape Town to Springbok is about R240–

R280 and Cape Town to Windhoek about R380–R450. It's about R120–R160 to George and R400–R450 to Durban. The Baz Bus hop-on/hop-off trip to Durban is about R930–R1,000 and is valid for about a year.

▶ BUS INFORMATION: **Baz Bus** (tel. 021/439–2323, fax 021/439–2343, www.bazbus.co.za). **Greyhound** (1 Adderley St., tel. 021/418–4310; 083/909–0909 for Computicket, www.greyhound.co.za). **Intercape Mainliner** (1 Adderley St., tel. 021/386–4400; 083/909–0909 for Computicket, www.intercape.co.za). **Translux Express Bus** (1 Adderley St., tel. 021/449–3333).

Bus Travel within Cape Town

Use the waterfront shuttle, as all the others are very slow and infrequent. It runs about every 10 minutes and costs about R4. Local minibus taxis tear around town at high speed, stuffed to capacity with hapless commuters. These buses ply routes all over the city and suburbs, but you can flag them down anywhere along the way. The depot is above the train station. For the modest fare of R5–R10 you can experience some local atmosphere and incidentally get to where you're going quite efficiently—although far from elegantly.

Car Rental

Most large car-rental agencies have offices in the city and at the airport and offer similar rates; expect to pay through the nose if you rent by the day. A Nissan Sentra or Toyota Corolla with a radio and tape player, automatic transmission, and air-conditioning costs about R220–R350 per day including 200 km (120 mi), plus R2.50–R3.00 for each additional kilometer. A no-frills Volkswagen Golf or Opel Corsa will cost you about R150–R200 per day, also including 200 km (120 mi), plus R1.05–R2.00 for each additional kilometer—these cars have manual transmission only. If you rent for five days or more, you could get unlimited kilometers. The quoted prices include insurance that covers 75%–90% of liability costs, but you can pay extra for 100% coverage.

It's best to deal with the car rental offices in Cape Town or at the airport (as opposed to those in smaller towns). If you're already in the Winelands and would like a car for the day, try Wine Route Rent-a-Car, based in Paarl, which will drop off a car at your hotel. The least stressful and most stylish way to tour the Winelands is by limo (about R350–R400 per hour per limo). It's particularly cost effective if you have a group of four or five.

➤ **MAJOR AGENCIES: Avis** (123 Strand St., tel. 021/424–1177; 021/934–0808 at the airport; 0800/002–1111 toll-free, www.avis.co.za). **Budget** (120 Strand St., tel. 021/418–5232; 021/934–0216 at the airport, www.budget.co.za). **Cape Limo Services** (tel. 021/785–3100). **Europcar** (tel. 021/418–0670, www.europcar.co.za). **Hertz** (40 Loop St., tel. 021/425–8251, www.hertz.co.za). **Wine Route Rent-a-Car** (tel. 021/872–8513 or 083/225–7089, www.encounter.co.za/rentacar).

INSURANCE
When driving a rented car you are generally responsible for any damage to or loss of the vehicle. You may also be liable for any property damage or personal injury that you may cause while driving. Before you rent, see what coverage you already have under the terms of your personal auto-insurance policy and credit cards.

REQUIREMENTS AND RESTRICTIONS
To rent a car, you must be over 25 years old and have a minimum of five years' driving experience. In South Africa your own driver's license is acceptable. An International Driver's Permit is a good idea; it's available from the American or Canadian Automobile Association or, in the United Kingdom, from the Automobile Association or Royal Automobile Club.

Car Travel

Parking in the city center can be a hassle. Parking spaces are so scarce that most hotels charge extra for the service, and even then you won't be guaranteed a space. You can usually find parking out on the Pay and Display lots on Buitengracht Street or on the Grand Parade. Wherever you park, you will be accosted by an informal (or semiformal) parking attendant. It's a good idea to pay him a rand in advance and then another rand or two if you return to find your car safe. The Sanlam Golden Acre Parking Garage, on Adderley Street, offers covered parking, as does the Parkade, on Strand Street.

However, outside of the city, driving yourself is undoubtedly the best way to appreciate the Western Cape area. The roads are generally good, although some dirt roads may be a bit rutted and bumpy. The wine route is easy to drive around, but of course driving limits the amount of wine you can taste, so unless you have a designated driver, it's best to take a tour, take a taxi, or— do it in style—rent a limo.

The main arteries leading out of the city are the N1, which runs to Paarl and, ultimately, Johannesburg; and the N2, which heads to the Overberg, the Garden Route, Eastern Cape, and, ultimately, Durban. The N7 goes up to Namibia and leads off the N1. The M3 (colloquially and rather loosely referred to as the Top Highway, the Top Freeway, or the Blue Route) leads to Constantia, Muizenberg, and the small towns of the peninsula; it splits from the N2 just after Groote Schuur Hospital, in the shadow of Devil's Peak.

EMERGENCY SERVICES

The Automobile Association of South Africa extends privileges to members of the American Automobile Association in the United States and the Automobile Association in Britain. Contact a local office in your home country for more information.

> **CONTACTS: Automobile Association of South Africa** (Box 31017, Braamfontein, Johannesburg 2017, tel. 011/799–1000 in Johannesburg; 021/419–6914 in Cape Town; 031/201–5244 in Durban; 080/001–0101 for 24-hr toll-free emergency).

GASOLINE

Huge 24-hour service stations are positioned at regular intervals along all major highways in South Africa, Botswana, and Namibia. Self-service stations do not exist, so an attendant will pump the gas, check the oil and water, and wash the windows. In return, tip him or her R2–R3. South Africa now has a choice of unleaded or leaded gasoline, and many vehicles operate on diesel—be sure you get the right fuel. Some South African–manufactured automobiles still need special engine modifications to enable them to run on unleaded fuel—check when booking a rental car as to what fuel to use. Gasoline is measured in liters, and expect to pay the equivalent of US$2–US$2.50 a gallon.

RULES OF THE ROAD

Southern Africans drive on the left. For pedestrians that means **look right before crossing the street.** South African roads have wide shoulders, separated from the main lanes by a yellow line. Slow traffic is expected to pull onto this shoulder to allow faster traffic to pass, but be sure that the shoulder ahead is not obstructed by cyclists, pedestrians, or a stopped vehicle. If a slower vehicle pulls onto the shoulder to allow you past, it's common courtesy to flash your hazard lights a couple of times in thanks. In built-up areas road shoulders are occasionally marked by red lines. This is a strict "no-stopping" zone.

Many cities use mini–traffic circles in lieu of four-way stops. These are extremely dangerous because many drivers don't bother to stop. In theory, the first vehicle to the circle has right-of-way; otherwise, yield to the right. In practice, keep your wits about you at all times.

In South African parlance, traffic lights are known as "robots," and what people refer to as the "pavement" is actually the sidewalk. Paved roads are just called roads. And for Americans and Canadians, don't forget: **drive left, and look right.**

Children in Cape Town

If you are renting a car, don't forget to **arrange for a car seat** when you reserve. For general advice about traveling with children, consult *Fodor's FYI: Travel with Your Baby* (available in bookstores everywhere).

FLYING

If your children are two or older, **ask about children's airfares.** As a general rule, infants under two not occupying a seat fly at greatly reduced fares or even for free. When booking, **confirm carry-on allowances** if you're traveling with infants. In general, for babies charged 10% of the adult fare you are allowed one carry-on bag and a collapsible stroller; if the flight is full, the stroller may have to be checked or you may be limited to less.

Experts agree that it's a good idea to use safety seats aloft for children weighing less than 40 pounds. Airlines set their own policies: U.S. carriers usually require that the child be ticketed, even if he or she is young enough to ride free, since the seats must be strapped into regular seats. Do **check your airline's policy about using safety seats during takeoff and landing.** Safety seats are not allowed everywhere in the plane, so get your seat assignments as early as possible.

When reserving, **request children's meals or a freestanding bassinet** (not available at all airlines) if you need them. But note that bulkhead seats, where you must sit to use the bassinet, may lack an overhead bin or storage space on the floor.

LODGING

Some luxury hotels do not accept children under 10 or 12 without prior arrangement, and many other hotels require children to eat dinner at a separate, earlier seating. Some hotels allow children under a certain age to stay in their parents' room at no extra charge, but others charge for them as extra adults; be sure to **find out the cutoff age for children's discounts.**

Southern Sun, the giant hotel group that operates Southern Sun and Holiday Inn properties throughout the country, allows children under 18 to stay free if sharing with parents in select hotels.

➤ **BEST CHOICES: Southern Sun** (tel. 011/482–3500).

SIGHTS AND ATTRACTIONS
Places that are especially appealing to children are indicated by a rubber-duckie icon (🦆) in the margin.

Customs and Duties

When shopping abroad, **keep receipts** for all purchases. Upon reentering the country, **be ready to show customs officials what you've bought.** If you feel a duty is incorrect, appeal the assessment. If you object to the way your clearance was handled, note the inspector's badge number. In either case, first ask to see a supervisor. If the problem isn't resolved, write to the appropriate authorities, beginning with the port director at your point of entry.

IN AUSTRALIA
Australian residents who are 18 or older may bring home A$400 worth of souvenirs and gifts (including jewelry), 250 cigarettes or 250 grams of tobacco, and 1,125 ml of alcohol (including wine, beer, and spirits). Residents under 18 may bring back A$200 worth of goods. Prohibited items include meat products. Seeds, plants, and fruits need to be declared upon arrival.

➤ **INFORMATION: Australian Customs Service** (Regional Director, Box 8, Sydney, NSW 2001, tel. 02/9213–2000, fax 02/9213–4000, www.customs.gov.au).

IN CANADA

Canadian residents who have been out of Canada for at least seven days may bring in C$750 worth of goods duty-free. If you've been away fewer than seven days but more than 48 hours, the duty-free allowance drops to C$200; if your trip lasts 24 to 48 hours, the allowance is C$50. You may not pool allowances with family members. Goods claimed under the C$750 exemption may follow you by mail; those claimed under the lesser exemptions must accompany you. Alcohol and tobacco products may be included in the seven-day and 48-hour exemptions but not in the 24-hour exemption. If you meet the age requirements of the province or territory through which you reenter Canada, you may bring in, duty-free, 1.5 liters of wine or 1.14 liters (40 imperial ounces) of liquor or 24 12-ounce cans or bottles of beer or ale. If you are 19 or older you may bring in, duty-free, 200 cigarettes and 50 cigars. Check ahead of time with the Canada Customs and Revenue Agency or the Department of Agriculture for policies regarding meat products, seeds, plants, and fruits.

You may send an unlimited number of gifts (only one gift per recipient, however) worth up to C$60 each duty-free to Canada. Label the package UNSOLICITED GIFT—VALUE UNDER $60. Alcohol and tobacco are excluded.

➤ **INFORMATION: Canada Customs and Revenue Agency** (2265 St. Laurent Blvd. S, Ottawa, Ontario K1G 4K3, tel. 204/983–3500 or 506/636–5064; 800/461–9999 in Canada, www.ccra-adrc.gc.ca).

IN NEW ZEALAND

All homeward-bound residents may bring back NZ$700 worth of souvenirs and gifts; passengers may not pool their allowances, and children can claim only the concession on goods intended for their own use. For those 17 or older, the duty-free allowance also includes 4.5 liters of wine or beer; one 1,125-ml bottle of spirits; and either 200 cigarettes, 250 grams of tobacco, 50 cigars, or a combination of the three up to 250 grams. Meat products, seeds, plants, and fruits must be declared upon arrival to the Agricultural Services Department.

➤ **INFORMATION: New Zealand Customs** (Head Office, The Customhouse, 17-21 Whitmore St., Box 2218, Wellington, tel. 09/ 300–5399, www.customs.govt.nz).

IN THE U.K.

From countries outside the European Union, including South Africa, you may bring home, duty-free, 200 cigarettes or 50 cigars; 1 liter of spirits or 2 liters of fortified or sparkling wine or liqueurs; 2 liters of still table wine; 60 ml of perfume; 250 ml of toilet water; plus £145 worth of other goods, including gifts and souvenirs. Prohibited items include meat products, seeds, plants, and fruits.

➤ **INFORMATION: HM Customs and Excise** (St. Christopher House, Southwark, London, SE1 OTE, tel. 020/7928–3344, www.hmce.gov.uk).

IN THE U.S.

U.S. residents who have been out of the country for at least 48 hours (and who have not used the $400 allowance or any part of it in the past 30 days) may bring home $400 worth of foreign goods duty-free; the duty-free allowance drops to $200 for fewer than 48 hours.

U.S. residents 21 and older may bring back 1 liter of alcohol duty-free. In addition, regardless of your age, you are allowed 200 cigarettes and 100 non-Cuban cigars. Antiques, which the U.S. Customs Service defines as objects more than 100 years old, enter duty-free, as do original works of art done entirely by hand, including paintings, drawings, and sculptures. You may also send packages home duty-free, with a limit of one parcel per addressee per day (except alcohol or tobacco products or perfume worth more than $5). You can mail up to $200 worth of goods for personal use; label the package PERSONAL USE and attach a list of its contents and their retail value. If the package contains your used personal belongings, mark it PERSONAL GOODS RETURNED to avoid paying duties. You may send up to $100 worth of goods as a gift; mark the package UNSOLICITED GIFT. Mailed items do not affect your duty-free allowance on your return.

➤ **INFORMATION: U.S. Customs Service** (for inquiries, 1300 Pennsylvania Ave. NW, Washington, DC 20229, tel. 202/354–1000, www.customs.gov; for complaints, Customer Satisfaction Unit, 1300 Pennsylvania Ave. NW, Room 5.5A, Washington, DC 20229; for registration of equipment, Office of Passenger Programs, 1300 Pennsylvania Ave. NW, Room 5.4D, Washington, DC 20229, tel. 202/927–0530).

Disabilities and Accessibility

South Africa is slowly adding facilities for travelers with disabilities, but standards vary widely from place to place. Many large chains now offer one or more rooms in their hotels specially adapted for travelers with disabilities.

LODGING

When discussing accessibility with an operator or reservations agent, **ask hard questions.** Are there any stairs, inside or out? Are there grab bars next to the toilet *and* in the shower/tub? How wide is the doorway to the room? To the bathroom? For the most extensive facilities meeting the latest legal specifications, **opt for newer accommodations.** If you reserve through a toll-free number, consider also calling the hotel's local number to confirm the information from the central reservations office. Get confirmation in writing when you can.

➤ **COMPLAINTS: Aviation Consumer Protection Division** (☞ Air Travel, *above*) for airline-related problems. **Departmental Office of Civil Rights** (for general inquiries, U.S. Department of Transportation, S-30, 400 7th St. SW, Room 10215, Washington, DC 20590, tel. 202/366–4648, fax 202/366–9371, www.dot.gov/

ost/docr/index.htm). **Disability Rights Section** (U.S. Department of Justice, Civil Rights Division, Box 66738, Washington, DC 20035-6738, tel. 202/514–0301 or 800/514–0301, or 800/514–0383 TTY, for ADA inquiries; www.usdoj.gov/crt/ada/adahom1.htm).

TRAVEL AGENCIES

In the United States, the Americans with Disabilities Act requires that travel firms serve the needs of all travelers. In South Africa, Flamingo Tours specialize in working with people with disabilities.

➤ **TRAVELERS WITH MOBILITY PROBLEMS: Access Adventures** (206 Chestnut Ridge Rd., Scottsville, NY 14624, tel. 716/889-9096), run by a former physical-rehabilitation counselor. **CareVacations** (No. 5, 5110–50 Ave., Leduc, Alberta T9E 6V4, Canada, tel. 780/986–6404 or 877/478–7827, fax 780/986–8332, www.carevacations.com), for group tours and cruise vacations. **Flamingo Tours** (Box 60554, Flamingo Sq., Cape Town 7441 South Africa, tel. 27/21/557–4496 or 27/82/420–2031, fax 27/21/557–4496, www.flamingotours.co.za). **Flying Wheels Travel** (143 W. Bridge St., Box 382, Owatonna, MN 55060, tel. 507/451–5005 or 800/535–6790, fax 507/451–1685, www.flyingwheelstravel.com).

Electricity

To use electric-powered equipment purchased in the United States or Canada, **bring a converter and adapter.** The electrical current is 220 volts, 50 cycles alternating current (AC); wall outlets in most of the region take 15-amp plugs with three round prongs (the old British system), but some take the straight-edged three-prong plugs, also 15 amps. If your appliances are dual-voltage, you'll need only an adapter. Don't use 110-volt outlets marked FOR SHAVERS ONLY for high-wattage appliances such as blow-dryers. Most laptops operate equally well on 110 and 220 volts and so require only an adapter.

Embassies and Consulates

➤ **AUSTRALIA: Australian High Commission** (Thibault Sq., BP Centre, 14th floor, tel. 021/419–5425, fax 021/419–7345).

➤ **CANADA: Canadian High Commission** (Reserve Bank Bldg., 19th floor, St. George's Mall, tel. 021/423–5240, fax 021/423–4893).

➤ **UNITED KINGDOM: British Consulate** (8 Riebeeck St., tel. 021/405–2400).

➤ **UNITED STATES: U.S. Consulate** (Broadway Bldg., Heerengracht [bottom of Adderley St.], tel. 021/421–4280, fax 021/425–4151, www.usembassy.state.gov/southafrica).

Emergencies

Dail 10177 for an ambulance and 10111 for the police. From a mobile phone, dial 112 in an emergency. Consult the front page of the local telephone directories for emergency numbers not listed here.

The police operate a Tourist Assistance Unit for foreign visitors who are robbed or experience other trouble. Medical Rescue International (MRI) offers professional evacuation in the event of real emergency. Divers Alert Network (DAN) is operated through MRI and can be accessed through MRI.

Public hospital emergency rooms have good service, but they are hopelessly understaffed and underfunded and have to deal with a huge number of local people, most of whom cannot afford any other alternative. If you can, contact one of the private clinics; make sure that you have overseas medical insurance that's good in South Africa before you leave home.

➤ **EMERGENCY SERVICES: Ambulance** (tel. 10177). **Fire** (tel. 10111). **Medical Rescue International** (MRI; tel. 27/11/242–0111;

0800/111–9990 in South Africa). **Police** (tel. 10111). **Tourist Assistance Unit** (Tulbagh Sq., tel. 021/421–5115).

➤ **HOSPITALS: City Park Hospital** (181 Longmarket St., tel. 021/480–6111). **Claremont Hospital;** Harfield and Main Rds., Claremont, tel. 021/670–4300). **Constantiaberg Medi-clinic** (Boundary Rd., Diep River, tel. 021/799–2911). **Newlands Surgical Clinic** (Pick and Pay Center, corner Main Rd. and Keurboom Rd., Claremont, tel. 021/683–1220). **Panorama Medi-clinic** (Rothchild Blvd., Panorama, tel. 021/938–2111).

➤ **HOT LINES: Ambulance** (tel. 10177). **Police** (tel. 10111).

Gay and Lesbian Travel

Cape Town is gay-friendly and has a very large gay population. The Gay and Lesbian Association of Cape Town Tourism, Industry, and Commerce (GALACTTIC) Web site (www.galacttic.co.za) lists gay-friendly hotels, restaurants, bars, clubs, events, and tours.

➤ **GAY- AND LESBIAN-FRIENDLY TRAVEL AGENCIES: Africa Outing** (5 Alcyone Rd., Claremont, Cape Town, South Africa 7708, tel. 27/21/671–4028 or 27/83/361–1255, fax 27/21/683–7377, www.afouting.com). **Different Roads Travel** (8383 Wilshire Blvd., Suite 902, Beverly Hills, CA 90211, tel. 323/651–5557 or 800/429–8747, fax 323/651–3678). **Kennedy Travel** (314 Jericho Turnpike, Floral Park, NY 11001, tel. 516/352–4888 or 800/237–7433, fax 516/354–8849, www.kennedytravel.com). **Now Voyager** (4406 18th St., San Francisco, CA 94114, tel. 415/626–1169 or 800/255–6951, fax 415/626–8626, www.nowvoyager.com). **Skylink Travel and Tour** (1006 Mendocino Ave., Santa Rosa, CA 95401, tel. 707/546–9888 or 800/225–5759, fax 707/546–9891, www.skylinktravel.com), serving lesbian travelers.

Health

During summer ticks may be found in open areas close to the city. If you intend to walk or hike anywhere, use a suitable insect repellent. After your walk examine your body and clothes for ticks, looking carefully for pepper ticks, which are tiny but just as virulent as their parents and can cause tick-bite fever. If you find a tick has bitten you, do not pull it off. If you do, you may pull the body off, and the head will remain embedded in your skin, causing an infection. Rather, smother the area with petroleum jelly, and the tick will eventually let go, as it will be unable to breathe; you can then scrape it off with a fingernail. If you are bitten, keep an eye on the bite. If the tick was infected, the bite will swell, itch, and develop a black necrotic center—this is a sure sign that you will develop tick-bite fever, which usually hits after about 8–12 days. Symptoms may be mild or severe, depending on the patient. This disease is not usually life threatening in healthy adults, but it is horribly unpleasant.

South Africa has no national health system, so check your existing health plan to see whether you're covered while abroad and supplement it if necessary. South African doctors are generally excellent. The equipment and training in private clinics rivals the best in the world, but public hospitals tend to suffer from overcrowding and underfunding.

MEDICAL PLANS

No one plans to get sick while traveling, but it happens, so consider signing up with a medical-assistance company. Members get doctor referrals, emergency evacuation or repatriation, hot lines for medical consultation, cash for emergencies, and other assistance.

➤ **MEDICAL-ASSISTANCE COMPANIES: International SOS Assistance** (www.internationalsos.com; 8 Neshaminy Interplex, Suite 207, Trevose, PA 19053, tel. 215/245–4707 or 800/523–6586, fax 215/244–9617; 12 Chemin Riantbosson, 1217 Meyrin 1, Geneva,

Switzerland, tel. 4122/785–6464, fax 4122/785–6424; 331 N. Bridge Rd., 17-00, Odeon Towers, Singapore 188720, tel. 65/338–7800, fax 65/338–7611).

SHOTS AND MEDICATIONS

No shots are required for travel to South Africa from the U.S., U.K., Australia, or New Zealand. However, the South African travel clinics and the U.S.'s National Centers for Disease Control (CDC) recommend that you be vaccinated against hepatitis A and hepatitis B if you intend to travel to isolated areas. If you plan to visit remote regions or stay for more than six weeks, check with the CDC's traveler's health line.

➤ HEALTH WARNINGS: National Centers for Disease Control and Prevention (CDC; National Center for Infectious Diseases, Division of Quarantine, Traveler's Health Section, 1600 Clifton Rd. NE, M/S E-03, Atlanta, GA 30333, tel. 888/232–3228 general information; 877/394–8747 travelers' health line, fax 888/232–3299, www.cdc.gov).

Holidays

National holidays include New Year's Day (Jan. 1); Human Rights Day (Mar. 21); Good Friday (Fri. before Easter); Easter Sunday (Apr. 20, 2003; Apr. 11, 2004); Family Day (Mon. after Easter); Freedom Day (Apr. 27); Workers Day (May 1); Youth Day (June 16); National Women's Day (Aug. 9); Heritage Day (Sept. 24); Day of Reconciliation (Dec. 16); Christmas Day (Dec. 25); and Day of Goodwill (Dec. 26).

Language

English is the widely spoken, unofficial lingua franca, although road signs and other important markers often alternate between English and Afrikaans (South African Dutch). Be warned that street names often alternate between the English and Afrikaans names, so, for example, "Wale Street" and "Waal Straat" are the same road.

South African English is heavily influenced by Afrikaans and, to a lesser extent, by some local African languages. First-time visitors may have trouble understanding regional South African accents.

Mail and Shipping

The mail service in South Africa is not spectacularly reliable. Mail can take weeks to arrive, and money and other valuables are frequently stolen from letters and packages. You can buy stamps only at post offices, open weekdays 8:30–4:30 and Saturday 8–noon. Stamps for local use only, marked STANDARDISED POST, may be purchased from newsagents in booklets of 10 stamps. Federal Express and several other express-mail companies offer more reliable service, as does the new Fast Mail and Speed Courier services.

RECEIVING MAIL

The central post office in each city has a poste restante desk that can hold mail for you. Be sure the post office's mail code and your name are prominently displayed on all letters. Most hotels also accept faxes and express-mail deliveries addressed to their guests. If you have trouble retrieving your mail, ask the clerk to check under the initial of your first name (and any other). So, for example, check under J, R, and S if your name is John Robert Smith. The best place to receive mail is at an American Express office. The Cape Town office is open 8:30–5 Monday through Friday and 9–11 AM on Saturday.

➤ **MAIL SERVICE: American Express** (1st Fl., Thibault House, Thibault Square, Cape Town, Western Cape 8001, tel. 021/408-9700, fax 021/408-9743).

Money Matters

Because of inflation and currency fluctuations it's difficult to give exact prices. It's safe to say, though, that Cape Town is an extremely cheap destination for foreign visitors. With the weakness of South African currencies against major foreign currencies, visitors will find the cost of meals, hotels, and entertainment considerably lower than at home. Flights to South Africa and within the country itself however, are extremely expensive.

A fabulous bottle of South African wine costs about $10 (double or triple in a restaurant), and a meal at a prestigious restaurant won't set you back more than $40 per person. Double rooms in the finest hotels may cost $250 a night, but $75 is more than enough to secure high-quality lodging. Hotel rates are at their highest during peak season, November through March, when you can expect to pay anywhere from 50% to 90% more than in the off-season.

The following were sample costs at the time of writing: cup of coffee, $1; bottle of beer in a bar, $1; quarter roasted chicken with salad and drink at a fast-food restaurant, $4–$5; room-service sandwich in a hotel, $4–$7; 2-km (1-mi) taxi ride, $6–$8.

Prices quoted throughout the book are in local currency where possible. Some tourist destinations are priced in dollars. Prices throughout this guide are given for adults. Substantially reduced fees are almost always available for children and students with valid international student cards.

For information on taxes see Taxes, below.

ATMS

Before leaving home, **make sure that your credit cards have been programmed for ATM use in South Africa** (most South African ATMs take five-digit PIN numbers). Note that Discover is accepted mostly in the United States. Local bank cards often do not work overseas or may access only your checking account; **ask your bank about a MasterCard/Cirrus or Visa debit card,** which works like a bank card but can be used at any ATM displaying a MasterCard/Cirrus or Visa logo. These cards, too, may tap only your checking account; check with your bank about their policy.

CREDIT CARDS

Throughout this guide, the following abbreviations are used: **AE,** American Express; **DC,** Diners Club; **MC,** MasterCard; and **V,** Visa.

➤ **REPORTING LOST CARDS: Amex** (tel. 011/710–4747), **Diners Club** (tel. 021/686–1990 or 011/482–2203), **MasterCard** (tel. 080/099–0418 toll free), **Visa** (tel. 080/099–0475 toll free).

CURRENCY

The unit of currency in South Africa is the rand (R), with 100 cents (¢) equaling R1. Bills come in R10, R20, R50, R100, and R200 denominations, which are differentiated by color. Coins are minted in R5, R2, R1, 50¢, 20¢, 10¢, 5¢, 2¢, and 1¢ denominations.

CURRENCY EXCHANGE

At this writing, conversion rates were as follows: R11.43 to US$1; R9.96 to €1; R5.79 to A$1; and R4.74 to NZ$1.

For the most favorable rates, **change money through banks.** Although ATM transaction fees may be higher abroad than at home, ATM rates are excellent because they are based on wholesale rates offered only by major banks. You won't do as well at exchange booths in airports or rail and bus stations, in restaurants, or in stores. **Don't even think about changing money at your hotel.** The rates at most hotels are outrageous, and the city center is swamped with banks and bureaux de change that give much better rates. American Express's downtown office is open weekdays 8:30–5 and Saturday 9–noon; at the waterfront, weekdays 9–7 and weekends 9–5.

Rennies Travel's downtown office is open weekdays 8:30–5 and Saturday 9–noon. The waterfront location is open until 9 daily.

To avoid lines at airport exchange booths, **get a few rands before you leave home.**

To avoid administrative hassles, keep all foreign-exchange receipts until you leave the country, as you may need them as proof when changing any unspent local currency back into your own currency. You may not take more than R5,000 in cash out of South Africa. For more information, contact the **South African Reserve Bank** (Box 427, Pretoria 0001, tel. 012/313–3911).

➤ **EXCHANGE SERVICES: American Express** (Thibault Sq., tel. 021/408–9700; Shop 11A, Alfred Mall, tel. 021/419–3917, www.amex.co.za). **International Currency Express** (tel. 888/278–6628 for orders, www.foreignmoney.com). **Rennies Travel's** (2 St. George's Mall, tel. 021/418–1206; Upper Level, Victoria Wharf, Waterfront, tel. 021/418–3744). **Thomas Cook Currency Services** (tel. 800/287–7362 for telephone orders and retail locations, www.us.thomascook.com).

Passports and Visas

Citizens of the U.S., U.K., Canada, Australia, and New Zealand need only a valid passport to enter South Africa for visits of up to 90 days.

When traveling internationally, **carry your passport** even if you don't need one (it's always the best form of I.D.) and **make two photocopies of the data page** (one for someone at home and another for you, carried separately from your passport). If you lose your passport, promptly call the nearest embassy or consulate and the local police.

If you plan to travel across borders within Africa, you may need a reentry visa to get back into the country you just left.

U.S. passport applications for children under age 14 require consent from both parents or legal guardians; both parents must appear together to sign the application. If only one parent appears, he or she must submit a written statement from the other parent authorizing passport issuance for the child. A parent with sole authority must present evidence of it when applying; acceptable documentation includes the child's certified birth certificate listing only the applying parent, a court order specifically permitting this parent's travel with the child, or a death certificate for the nonapplying parent. Application forms and instructions are available on the Web site of the U.S. State Department's Bureau of Consular Affairs (www.travel.state.gov).

PASSPORT OFFICES

The best time to apply for a passport or to renew is in fall and winter. Before any trip, check your passport's expiration date, and, if necessary, renew it as soon as possible.

➤ **AUSTRALIAN CITIZENS: Australian State Passport Office** (tel. 131–232, www.dfat.gov.au/passports).

➤ **CANADIAN CITIZENS: Passport Office** (tel. 819/994–3500; 800/567–6868 in Canada, www.dfait-maeci.gc.ca/passport).

➤ **NEW ZEALAND CITIZENS: New Zealand Passport Office** (tel. 04/494–0700 or 04/474–8100 for application procedures, www.passports.govt.nz).

➤ **U.K. CITIZENS: London Passport Office** (tel. 0870/521–0410, www.ukpa.gov.uk) for application procedures and to request an emergency passport.

➤ **U.S. CITIZENS: National Passport Information Center** (tel. 900/225–5674; calls are 35¢ per minute for automated service, $1.05 per minute for operator service; www.travel.state.gov). **Office of Passport Services** (tel. 202/647–0518).

Safety

Crime is a major problem in Cape Town, and all visitors should take precautions to protect themselves. **Do not walk alone at night,** and exercise caution even during the day. Avoid wearing flashy jewelry or advertising an expensive camera and keep your belongings close to you at all times.

Carjacking is another problem, with armed bandits often forcing drivers out of their vehicles at traffic lights, in driveways, or during a fake accident. Keep your car doors locked at all times, and leave enough space between you and the vehicle in front so you can pull into another lane if necessary. If you are confronted by an armed assailant, do not resist. Because of the number of sophisticated antihijacking and vehicle-tracking devices, carjackers may try to force you off the road, so as to steal the car while the engine is running. Another possibility is being forced to accompany carjackers for some time, showing them where the hidden emergency switches are. If this happens, don't panic, scream, or otherwise draw attention to yourself. Follow instructions carefully, and do not attempt to try to remove your valuables or other items from the car—you'll have a far better chance of emerging from the experience unscathed.

Know exactly where you're going. Purchase a good map and obtain comprehensive directions. Taking the wrong exit off a highway into a township could lead you straight to disaster. Learn from your hotel or the locals which areas to avoid.

Never, ever visit a township or squatter camp on your own. Unemployment is rife, and obviously affluent foreigners are easy pickings. If you wish to see a township, check with reputable companies, which run excellent tours and know which areas to avoid. Book yourself on one of these instead.

The countryside is less intense and crime is not as common, but **always remain alert,** and **don't let a false sense of security lead** you into behaving foolishly. Most hiking trails and tourist areas are reasonably safe, but crime can and does happen anywhere.

Before your trip check with the U.S. State Department (tel. 202/647–5225, travel.state.gov) to see if there are any current advisories. But before you rush to cancel a trip, remember southern Africa is a very big place. Something happening in Zimbabwe will have no effect whatsoever on tourists in Cape Town. It really is worth your while to get good, up-to-date information from locals. Most tour operators would rather cancel a trip than risk a nasty incident, and they are usually in a good position to ascertain the real risks.

Senior-Citizen Travel

Senior citizens in South Africa often receive discounts on admission prices and tickets if they can show valid pensioner's cards, which prove they they are on a fixed income, as age itself is no indication of financial status. As a foreigner, though, you are unlikely to get a discount.

➤ EDUCATIONAL PROGRAM: Elderhostel (11 Ave. de Lafayette, Boston, MA 02111-1746, tel. 877/426–8056, fax 877/426–2166, www.elderhostel.org).

Taxes

HOTEL
South Africa levies a bed tax on hotels. It is usually included in the price quoted and is included in all prices listed in this book.

VALUE-ADDED TAX
In South Africa the value-added tax (VAT), currently a whopping 14%, is included in the price of most goods and services, including hotel accommodations and food. To get a VAT refund, foreign visitors must present their receipts (minimum of R250) at the airport and be carrying any purchased items with them or

in their luggage. You must fill out Form VAT 255, available at the airport VAT refund office. Whatever you buy, **make sure that your receipt is an original tax invoice, containing the vendor's name and address, VAT registration number, and the words *tax invoice*.** Refunds are paid by check, which can be cashed immediately at an airport bank. If you have packed your purchases in luggage you intend to check, be sure you visit the VAT refund desk before you go through check-in procedures. For items in your carry-on baggage, visit the refund desk in the departures hall.

Taxis

Taxis are metered and reasonably priced and offer an easy, quick way to get around a city where parking is such trouble. Don't expect to see the throngs of cabs you find in London or New York. You may be lucky enough to hail one on the street, but your best bet is to summon one by phone or head to a major taxi stand—Greenmarket Square and the top and bottom (opposite the station) of Adderley Street. Sea Point Taxis, probably the most reliable of the companies, starts the meter at R2 and charges R7 per kilometer. Waiting time is charged at about R50 an hour. Another reputable company is Marine Taxis. Expect to pay R40–R60 for a trip from the city center to the waterfront. In the Winelands, Paarl Radio Taxis transport up to three people at about R6 per kilometer (R9 per mile) and R30 per hour waiting time. Larger groups can arrange transportation by minibus.

➤ **TAXI COMPANIES: Marine Taxis** (tel. 021/434–0434). **Paarl Radio Taxis** (tel. 021/872–5671). **Sea Point Taxis** (tel. 021/434–4444).

Telephones

The phone system in Cape Town is good. A major difficulty is the high cost of scrap copper, so it's not unknown for a couple of miles of telephone cable to go missing overnight, leaving large areas incommunicado. Cell phones are ubiquitous and have quite extensive coverage. Your best, cheapest, and least complicated way of making and receiving phone calls is to **obtain international roaming service from your cell phone service provider before you leave home.** Cell phones can also be rented by the day, week, or longer from the airport on your arrival.

➤ **CELLULAR PHONE RENTAL: GSM** (Global System for Mobile Communications; tel. 021/934–4951 in Cape Town).

AREA AND COUNTRY CODES
The country code for South Africa is 27. When dialing from abroad, drop the initial 0 from the local area code. The country code is 1 for the United States and Canada, 61 for Australia, 64 for New Zealand, and 44 for the United Kingdom.

DIRECTORY AND OPERATOR ASSISTANCE
For directory assistance call tel. 1023 for local calls or tel. 1025 for national long-distance calls. For international operator assistance dial tel. 0903.

LOCAL CALLS
Local calls are very cheap, although all calls from hotels attract a hefty premium.

LONG-DISTANCE SERVICES
AT&T, MCI, and Sprint access codes make calling long distance relatively convenient, but you may find the local access number blocked in many hotel rooms. First ask the hotel operator to connect you. If the hotel operator balks, ask for an international operator, or dial the international operator yourself. One way to improve your odds of getting connected to your long-distance carrier is to travel with more than one company's calling card (a hotel may block Sprint, for example, but not MCI). If all else fails, call from a pay phone.

➤ **ACCESS CODES: AT&T Direct** (tel. 0800/99–0123). **MCI WorldPhone** (tel. 0800/990–011). **Sprint International Access** (tel. 0800/990–001).

PUBLIC PHONES AND PHONE CARDS

There are two types of pay phones: coin-operated phones and card-operated phones. Phone cards are available in several denominations and are useful as they free you from the hassle of juggling handfuls of coins. A digital readout tells you how much credit remains while you're talking. Telephone cards are available at newsagents, convenience stores, and telephone company offices.

Time

South Africa operates on CAST (Central African Standard Time), which is two hours ahead of Greenwich mean time. That makes it seven hours ahead of North American eastern standard time (six hours ahead during eastern daylight savings time).

Tipping

Tipping is an integral part of South African life, and tips are expected for services that you might take for granted at home. Most notable among these is when you fill up with gas; there are no self-service stations, and you should tip the attendant R2–R3 if he or she offers to clean your windshield, check your oil and water, and is generally helpful. In restaurants the size of the tip should depend on the quality of service, but 10% is standard, unless, of course, a service charge has already been added to the bill. Give the same percentage to bartenders, taxi drivers, and tour guides. Hotel porters should receive R1.50–R2 per bag. Informal parking attendants may look a bit seedy, but they do provide a good service, so tip them a couple of rand if your car is still in one piece when you return to it.

Tours

BOAT TOURS

Until the middle of the 20th century most travelers' first glimpse of Cape Town was from the sea, and that's still the best way to get a feeling for the city, with its famous mountain as a backdrop. Waterfront Charters offers a range of boats, ranging from sailing boats to large motor boats, and operates out of the Waterfront. A sunset cruise costs about R100. Drumbeat Charters does regular Seal Island trips that last about 40 minutes and cost about R35–R50. Tigger Too concentrates on more comfortable trips for smaller groups out of Hout Bay. It offers a lunch cruise (four hours, including three-course meal) for R370–R400 and a sunset cruise with snacks and sparkling wine for R155–R170.

Boat trips to Robben Island don't actually land on the famous island. If you want to tour the island where Nelson Mandela spent a good chunk of his life, you need to organize a tour through the Robben Island Museum.

➤ **FEES AND SCHEDULES: Drum Beat Charters** (tel. 021/438–9208). **Tigger Too Charters** (tel. 021/790–5256, www.tiggertoo.co.za). **Waterfront Charters** (tel. 021/418–0134, www.waterfrontcharters.co.za).

BUS TOURS

A host of companies offer guided tours of the city, the peninsula, the Winelands, and anyplace else in the Cape you might wish to visit. Hylton Ross, Classic Cape Tours, Mother City Tours, Welcome Tours and Safaris, and Springbok Atlas offer bus tours of all the major attractions in the Cape Town area. Prices range from about R180–R200 for a half-day trip to about R300–R350 for a full-day tour. If you're a little more adventurous, you may prefer an outing with Ferdinand's Tours—somewhat less staid than the run-of-the-mill tour. It does an excellent wine route trip that includes a visit to a shebeen (an unlicensed drinking establishment) as a contrast. An even more adventurous tour would be a bike/bus tour with the Baz Bus—it does the usual peninsula route with a trailer of bikes—you cycle the fun parts and sit in the bus for the in-between bits. If you're tired, you can just opt out of the cycling. It costs about R200.

Muse-Art Journeys conducts fascinating tours (about R160) covering the cultural life of Cape Town, including art, music, crafts, and architecture. The graffiti tour is a real eye-opener and includes an introduction to hip-hop art and music.

➤ FEES AND SCHEDULES: Baz Bus (tel. 021/439–2323, fax 021/439–2343, www.bazbus.com). Classic Cape Tours (tel. 021/686–6310, fax 021/686–9216, www.classiccape.co.za). Ferdinand's Tours (tel. 021/465–8550 or 083/462–0425, fax 021/448–0003, www.ferdinandstours.co.za). Hylton Ross Tours (tel. 021/511–1784, fax 021/511–2401, www.hyltonross.co.za). Mother City Tours (tel. 021/448–3817, fax 021/448–3844, www.mctours.co.za). Muse-Art Journeys (tel. 021/919–9168). Springbok Atlas (tel. 021/460–4700, www.springbokatlas.com). Welcome Tours & Safaris (tel. 021/510–6001, fax 021/510–6023, www.welcome.co.za).

HELICOPTER TOURS
Court Helicopters and Civair Helicopters offer tours of the city and surrounding area ranging in length from 20 minutes to several hours. Custom tours can be arranged.

➤ FEES AND SCHEDULES: CHC Helicopters (Africa) (Waterfront, tel. 021/425–2966). Civair Helicopters (Waterfront, tel. 021/419–5182, www.civair.co.za).

WALKING TOURS
Legend Tours offers Walk to Freedom tours that cover District Six, Bo-Kaap, the townships, and Robben Island. The well-informed guides lead the tours, casting a strong historical and political emphasis.

➤ **FEES AND SCHEDULES: Legend Tours** (tel. 021/697–4056, fax 021/697–4090, www.legendtourism.co.za).

WINELANDS TOURS

Ferdinand's Tours offers fun and funky Wineland tours for decidedly young-at-heart travelers. More conservative tour companies include the reliable standbys Springbok Atlas, Welcome Tours & Safaris, and Hylton Ross. If you're serious about wine, Vineyard Ventures is the best of several companies offering tours of the Winelands. Sisters Gillian Stoltzman and Glen Christie are knowledgeable and passionate about wine and tailor tours to your interests. The cost ranges from R600 per person for four people to R1,500 for one person and includes all tastings, museum entries, and a fabulous lunch (with wine, of course).

➤ **FEES AND SCHEDULES: Ferdinand's Tours** (tel. 021/465–8550 or 083/462–0425, www.ferdinandstours.co.za). **Hylton Ross Tours** (tel. 021/511–1784, www.hyltonross.co.za). **Springbok Atlas** (tel. 021/460–4700, www.springbokatlas.com). **Vineyard Ventures** (5 Hanover Rd., Fresnaye, Cape Town 8001, tel. 021/434–8888 or 082/920–2825, www.vineyardventures.co.za). **Welcome Tours & Safaris** (tel. 021/510–6001, www.welcome.co.za).

Train Travel

Cape Town's train station is in the heart of the city, and there are a number of trains that operate from the station, including the *Trans-Karoo*, *Southern Cross* (which is a night ride, so forget about seeing the splendors of the Garden Route), the *Union Limited Steam Train*, the luxury *Blue Train*, and the luxurious *Rovos Rail Pride of Africa*, which also travels from Cape Town to Johannesburg and up the Garden Route.

Cape Metro is Cape Town's commuter line and offers regular but infrequent service to the southern suburbs and the towns on the False Bay side of the peninsula, including Muizenberg, St. James, Kalk Bay, Fish Hoek, and Simonstown.

All trains depart from Cape Town station on Adderley Street. Cape Metro also serves Paarl, Stellenbosch, and Somerset West, in the Winelands, but with the increase in violent muggings and robberies in the area, the trains should be avoided. A far safer, more stylish, and more fun alternative would be to hop on the Spier Train when it is running. Regular trips run from Spier Monument Station out to Spier, in the Winelands, at R75 for a round-trip.

If you travel on the Metro train during off-peak periods, choose as crowded a compartment as you can, and be alert to your surroundings when the train is stopped at a station, as agile young bag-snatchers can slip in and out pretty quickly and target "dreamy" passengers or those engrossed in a book. Strange as it sounds, you may be safer standing in a cramped third-class carriage than sitting comfortably in splendid isolation in an empty first-class one.

FARES AND SCHEDULES

Mainline Passenger Services' *Trans-Karoo* runs daily between Cape Town and Johannesburg; the trip takes about 25 hours and costs about R400 first-class. The *Southern Cross* makes the 24-hour trip to Port Elizabeth on Friday and back on Sunday (R235 first-class). The *Blue Train* makes the Cape Town–Johannesburg run three times per week and the Cape Town–Port Elizabeth run once a month. Depending on the compartment, time of year, and route, the trip can cost anywhere between R4,000 and R20,000. The Rovos Rail trip from Cape Town to Pretoria costs between R7,500 and R1,000. The Cape Metro trip to False Bay takes 45–60 minutes and costs about R20 for a one-way first-class ticket. The trains do not run after 7 PM during the week or after about 2 PM on Saturday. There is one train an hour between about 7:30 and 11 and between 3:30 and 7:30 on Sunday.

➤ **TRAIN INFORMATION: Blue Train** (tel. 021/449–2672, www.bluetrain.co.za). **Cape Metro** (tel. 080/065–6463). **Cape Town train station** (Cape Town station, Adderley St., tel. 021/449–3871). *Rovos Rail Pride of Africa* (tel. 021/421–4020, www.rovos.co.za). **Spier Train** (tel. 021/419–5222, www.spier.co.za).

RESERVATIONS
The reservations office at the Cape Town station is open Monday–Thursday 8–4:30, Friday 8–4, and Saturday 8–noon.

Transportation Around Cape Town

If you confine yourself to the city center, you won't need a car—in fact, the shortage of parking spaces makes having a car in the city a nightmare. A fun and practical option is to rent a scooter (which eliminates parking problems) from African Buzz for R160–R200 per day for unlimited kilometers, or a motorcycle from Mitaka for R350–R450 per day, which includes 300 km (180 mi) (thereafter, about R1 per kilometer).

➤ **MOTORCYCLE/SCOOTER RENTAL: African Buzz** (Long St., tel. 021/423–0052, fax 021/423–0056). **Mitaka** (Sea Point, tel. 021/439–6036, www.mitaka.co.za).

Travel Agencies

A good travel agent puts your needs first. Look for an agency that has been in business at least five years, emphasizes customer service, and has someone on staff who specializes in your destination. In addition, **make sure the agency belongs to a professional trade organization.** The American Society of Travel Agents (ASTA)—the largest and most influential in the field with more than 26,000 members in some 170 countries—maintains and enforces a strict code of ethics and will step in to help mediate any agent-client disputes involving ASTA members if necessary. ASTA (whose motto is "Without a travel agent, you're on your own") also maintains a Web site that includes a directory of agents. (If a travel agency is also acting as your tour operator, *see* Buyer Beware in Tours and Packages, *above*.)

➤ **LOCAL AGENT REFERRALS: American Society of Travel Agents** (ASTA; 1101 King St., Suite 200, Alexandria, VA 22314 tel. 800/965–2782 24-hr hot line, fax 703/739–7642, www.astanet.com). **Association of British Travel Agents** (68–71 Newman St., London W1T 3AH, U.K., tel. 020/7637–2444, fax 020/7637–0713, www. abtanet.com). **Association of Canadian Travel Agents** (130 Albert St., Suite 1705, Ottawa, Ontario K1P 5G4, Canada, tel. 613/237–3657, fax 613/237–7052, www.acta.net). **Australian Federation of Travel Agents** (Level 3, 309 Pitt St., Sydney NSW 2000, Australia, tel. 02/9264–3299, fax 02/9264–1085, www.afta.com.au). **Travel Agents' Association of New Zealand** (Level 5, Tourism and Travel House, 79 Boulcott St., Box 1888, Wellington 10033, New Zealand, tel. 04/499–0104, fax 04/499–0827, www.taanz.org.nz).

Videos and Books

VIDEOS

Most movies about South Africa have traditionally focused on the tragedy of apartheid. Well worth watching is the remake of *Cry, the Beloved Country* (1995), starring James Earl Jones. *Cry Freedom* (1987), starring Denzel Washington and Kevin Kline, follows the story of white South African jounalist Donald Woods and Steve Biko, a prominent black activist who died in 1977 after being beaten in police custody in Port Elizabeth. *Breaker Morant* (1979), a superbly crafted and acted Australian movie about the Anglo–Boer War (1899–1902), looks at British military hypocrisy through the eyes of three Australian soldiers on trial for shooting Boer prisoners.

The South African movie industry, although in its relative infancy, has produced one major hit, *The Gods Must Be Crazy* (1980), the enchanting story of a San clan in the Kalahari Desert. Try to get your hands on the 1980s movie version of *Jock of the Bushveld*, starring Jonathan Rand, with music by Johhny Clegg and

Savuka—it's delightful. Gavin Hood's fine movie *A Reasonable Man* (1999) tells the story of a simple Zulu cowherd on trial for killing a child whom he believed to be an evil spirit. With a superb performance by Sir Nigel Hawthorne as the trial judge, this groundbreaking and thought-provoking movie, based on an actual case in South African law, attempts to answer the questions: Who is a reasonable man? Which standards do we apply—those of Western law or traditional African belief? And which, if either, is right?

BOOKS

Long Walk to Freedom, by Nelson Mandela is an inspiring account of the triumph of idealism. The book looks back over Mandela's life and also takes a pragmatic view of the political road ahead—it should be required reading for South Africans and visitors alike. A more accessible read, illustrated with striking photographs, is the shortened version, *The Illustrated Long Walk to Freedom*.

Rainbow People of God tells the story of another of the heroes of the struggle, Archbishop Desmond Tutu, through his speeches, sermons, and letters from 1976 to 1994. His recent and poignant personal account of the proceedings, stories, and people he presided over as chairman of the Truth and Reconciliation Commission (TRC) is remarkable for its sense of balance and lack of bitterness, in spite of the accounts of the horrors and trauma he heard on a daily basis for many months. His compassion and willingness to forgive mirror Nelson Mandela's own remarkable positive attitudes toward the past.

For a lyrical, impassioned, and disturbing account of the TRC hearings, try poet Antje Krog's *Country of My Skull*. *Mandela: The Authorized Biography*, Anthony Sampson, is the definitive biography of the man who changed South African politics, assessing the years before, during, and after his imprisonment.

More required, and compulsive, reading for every visitor is *Indaba, My Children*, by Credo Mutwa, the most famous and best loved of all African *sangomas* (healers, prophets, and shamans). Described by the *London Sunday Times* as "a work of genius," it's an unputdownable compilation of African tribal history, legends, customs, and religious beliefs by a master storyteller.

A classic and very readable study of the San (Bushmen), Elizabeth Marshall Thomas's *The Harmless People* describes the traditional ways of this hunting-gathering culture, which has become endangered and made almost extinct by the intrusion of industrial civilization. Thomas Pakenham's reader-friendly, fascinating, and definitive study *The Boer War* explains an important and evocative part of South Africa's colonial history, when thousands of British soldiers died fighting for a cause they didn't understand in a country they barely knew. Their enemy? The brave independent Boers, the founders of fierce and innovative guerilla warfare, who were fighting for the fatherland they had carved out of the African wilderness.

South African writers have drawn steadily from the well of racial injustice to produce some of the finest literature of the 20th century. One of the first such novels is one of the best: Alan Paton's *Cry, the Beloved Country* (1948). Nadine Gordimer, who won the Nobel Prize for literature in 1991, is known both for her short stories and her novels. *The Conservationist* and *July's People* will give you insights into South Africa, its peoples, problems, and history. Other major writers include Booker Prize winner J. M. Coetzee (*Life and Times of Michael K*, *Waiting for the Barbarians*, *Disgrace*, and other books); Athol Fugard (*Master Harold and the Boys*, *Boesman and Lena*), South Africa's most famous playwright; and André Brink, whose accessible novels make for compulsive reading: Try his historical novel *A Chain of Voices* or the magical realism of *Devil's Valley* for a start.

A short-story writer who captured the slow, measured life of Afrikaner farmers and early settlers is Herman Charles Bosman. Laced with humor and irony, Bosman's stories recapture a time in South Africa when survival was a triumph and religion and peach brandy were necessary crutches.

Visitor Information

Cape Town Tourism is the city's official tourist body and offers information on tours, hotels, restaurants, rental cars, and shops. It also has a coffee shop, wine shop, and Internet café. The staff also makes hotel, tour, travel, and walking-tour reservations. It is open weekdays 9–6, Saturday 8:30–2, and Sunday 9–1. For information about traveling to and within South Africa, contact the nearest office of South African Tourism.

➤ **TOURIST INFORMATION: Cape Town Tourism** (The Pinnacle at Burg and Castle Sts. [Box 1403], 8000, tel. 021/426–4260, fax 021/426–4263, www.cape-town.org). **Franschhoek Vallée Tourismé** (Huguenot Rd., Franschhoek, tel. 021/876–3603). **Paarl Tourism Bureau** (216 Main St., Paarl, tel. 021/872–3829 or 021/872–4842, www.paarlonline.com). **South African Tourism, U.S.** (500 5th Ave., Suite 2040, New York, NY 10110, tel. 800/822–5368, fax 212/764–1980; 9841 Airport Blvd., Suite 1524, Los Angeles, CA 90045, tel. 800/782–9772, fax 310/641–5812). **South African Tourism, Canada** (4117 Lawrence Ave. E, Suite 2, Scarborough, Ontario M1E 2S2, tel. 416/283–0563, fax 416/283–5465). **South African Tourism** (Private Bag X164, Pretoria 0001, tel. 012/347–0600, fax 012/347–6199). **South African Tourism, U.K.** (5–6 Alt Grove, Wimbledon SW19 4DZ, tel. 0181/944–8080, fax 0181/944–6705). **Stellenbosch Tourist Bureau** (36 Market St., Stellenbosch, tel. 021/883–3584, fax 021/883–8017).

Web Sites

Do check out the World Wide Web when planning your trip. You'll find everything from weather forecasts to virtual tours. Be sure to visit **Fodors.com** (www.fodors.com), a complete travel-planning site. You can research prices and book plane tickets, hotel rooms, rental cars, vacation packages, and more. In addition, you can post your pressing questions in the Travel Talk section. Other planning tools include a currency converter and weather reports, and there are loads of links to travel resources.

For more information on Cape Town and the Cape Peninsula, visit www.southafrica.net, www.cape-town.org, www.capetourism.org, and www.gocapetown.co.za.

When to Go

As South Africa is in the southern hemisphere, its seasons are opposite to those in the northern hemisphere—it's summer there during the North American and European winter.

Peak tourist season is from November through March, when hotel prices rise dramatically and making a reservation can be difficult. The situation is exacerbated during major school holidays—especially December 1–January 15, the South African summer vacation—when South African families take to the roads in droves. Schools also have two weeks' vacation around Easter and a month in July or August.

The most popular time to visit Cape Town is from November through January, although February and March offer the best weather. Keep in mind, however, that the shoulder months of October and April can be fabulous and uncrowded. Cape winters (May–August) are notorious for cold, windy, rainy weather, but in reality these are miserable days interspersed with glorious sunny days that rival the best summer days in Britain. This season is known as the "secret season," during which really good deals can be had. As long as you stay for a week or more, you're bound to have at least a few days of gorgeous weather.

South Africa, like the rest of the world, has been experiencing erratic climate recently, so pack good rain gear wherever you go. **Take along a warm jacket, too.** It really and truly does get very cold here. Always bring shorts, T-shirts, sandals, a sun hat, and a swimsuit.

CLIMATE

The following are average daily maximum and minimum temperatures for Cape Town.

➤ **FORECASTS: Weather Channel Connection** (tel. 900/932–8437), 95¢ per minute from a Touch-Tone phone.

CAPE TOWN

Jan.	79F	26C	May	68F	20C	Sept.	66F	19C
	61	16		48	9		48	9
Feb.	81F	27C	June	64F	18C	Oct.	70F	21C
	61	16		46	8		52	11
Mar.	77F	25C	July	64F	18C	Nov.	75F	24C
	57	14		45	7		55	13
Apr.	73F	23C	Aug.	64F	18C	Dec.	77F	25C
	54	12		46	8		59	15

index

180

FODOR'S POCKET CAPE TOWN

EDITORS: Shannon Kelly, Melissa Klurman

Editorial Contributors: Andrew Barbour, Myrna Robins, Jennifer Stern

Editorial Production: Tom Holton

Maps: David Lindroth, *cartographer;* Bob Blake and Rebecca Baer, *map editors*

Design: Fabrizio La Rocca, *creative director;* Tigist Getachew, *art director;* Jolie Novak, *senior picture editor;* Melanie Marin, *photo editor*

Production/Manufacturing: Robert B. Shields

Cover Photograph: Hugh Sitton/ Stone

COPYRIGHT

First Edition

ISBN 0–676–90880–2

ISSN 1537–5587

IMPORTANT TIP

Although all prices, opening times, and other details in this book are based on information supplied to us at press time, changes occur all the time in the travel world, and Fodor's cannot accept responsibility for facts that become outdated or for inadvertent errors or omissions. So **always confirm information when it matters,** especially if you're making a detour to visit a specific place.

SPECIAL SALES

Fodor's Travel Publications are available at special discounts for bulk purchases for sales promotions or premiums. Special editions, including personalized covers, excerpts of existing guides, and corporate imprints, can be created in large quantities for special needs. For more information, contact your local bookseller or write to Special Markets, Fodor's Travel Publications, 280 Park Avenue, New York, NY 10017. Inquiries from Canada should be directed to your local Canadian bookseller or sent to Random House of Canada, Ltd., Marketing Department, 2775 Matheson Boulevard East, Mississauga, Ontario L4W 4P7. Inquiries from the United Kingdom should be sent to Fodor's Travel Publications, 20 Vauxhall Bridge Road, London SW1V 2SA, England.

PRINTED IN THE UNITED STATES OF AMERICA

10 9 8 7 6 5 4 3 2 1